Lessons
from the
Holy Wars

A Pakistani-American Odyssey

Rob Asghar

Lessons from the Holy Wars: A Pakistani-American Odyssey

Copyright © 2010 Rob Asghar. All rights reserved. No part of this book may be reproduced or retransmitted in any form or by any means without the written permission of the publisher.

Published by Wheatmark®
610 East Delano Street, Suite 104
Tucson, Arizona 85705 U.S.A.
www.wheatmark.com

International Standard Book Number: 978-1-60494-369-6
Library of Congress Control Number: 2009941901

Author contact information:
www.RobAsghar.com
RobAsghar@gmail.com

rev20091228

To my nieces Emaan, Zara and Natalie, and my nephew Nicholas, for bringing boundless, youthful joy into my life—without my needing to ever change one diaper.

Contents

Foreword by Warren Bennis . . . . *xi*

Introduction: "Who" Is Wise? . . . . *xv*

BOOK 1: A Pakistani-American Odyssey

I: There Appears to Be Only One God, Allah, and
Muhammad Is His Prophet. *3*
           *[Wherein the writer seeks to be a good immigrant son
and a typical American too, against all common sense.]*

A match made in heaven and a mud-hut village *3*
Father Knows Best? *3*
CULTURAL COLLISION 1: Brown man's burden. *4*
Saving sex, and handshakes, for marriage *5*
Ali & Harriet: the early days *6*
Less holy and more American than thou *7*
CULTURAL COLLISION 2: Hello, Pakistan, I hate you. *8*
Love cannot be bought *9*
A mother of a motherland *10*
Get a job, you lazy quadriplegics *10*
Twirling dervish *11*
A little slice of America called Tehran *12*

The Fonz Cometh 12
CULTURAL COLLISION 3:
Religious cartoons, without the rioting. 13
When a Charlie Brown Christmas looks relatively impressive 14
Can't judge a book by its unintelligent cover 15
Alex Haley only appreciated his roots because
he didn't have to live there 16
Be true to your high-security, diplomatic enclave school. 17
Sweeping poverty under the rug 18
CULTURAL COLLISION 4: Rob meets Bizarro Rob 20
CULTURAL COLLISION 5: "Death to America,"
the popular new game everyone's playing. 21
A pawn of the bomb-maker's daughter 24
Rambling on. 26
CULTURAL COLLISION 6: The coming of the godless communists,
and the beginning of the end of the
Pakistan we once knew 27
California Dreaming 28
Party like a verb. 29
CULTURAL COLLISION 7: Is there a *real* doctor in the house? ... 31
CULTURAL COLLISION 8: Let's not get *too* American 33

II: **Jesus Saves** 37
[Wherein the writer finds salvation and many other divinely sponsored aggravations, and visits those gifts upon an unwilling family.]

CULTURAL COLLISION 9: Jack & Coke & Dad & Me 37
The contest: no, not the Seinfeldian kind 38
Spiritual, not religious... yet. 41
Finding Jesus, and being outed for the trouble. 43

Happy Mother's Day... 45
CULTURAL COLLISION 10:
We don't care who the reason for the season is 46
Point, counterpointed—over and over 50
Second-worst man alive, with a bullet 51
You're brainwashed, I'm just well-informed 52
Meet the Mullah.. 53
Let my rivals tremble 54
Every sin is bigger in Texas 55
Going Hollywood, evangelical-style 57
Finding a place in the sun..................................... 58
Love, Pakistani-style and modern-style 59
Bizarro Rob meets Bizarro Krypton.......................... 60
In Tod we trust... 62
When the Lord gets too lenient 64
Make disciples of all nations, except the one you're from 65
Jesus Freak returns to Islamabad.............................. 67
You look good in a closet...................................... 68
Faith is only confusing when you think about it 70
They like me, they really like me 71
Rockin' with the Lord, vaguely................................ 73

III: The Gods Are Dead, or at Least Underachieving 76
[Wherein the writer, having peered into Heaven, chooses at last to return to earth and finds contentment there.]

Crazy for Jesus, or because of Jesus........................... 76
CULTURAL COLLISION 11:
The plane and skyscraper kind................................. 77
To prophet or profit?.. 80

Writer gains minor fame, hijinks ensue *82*
Mom & me & the Boss *84*
Is anything worse than apostasy? *85*
CULTURAL COLLISION 12: The Jihadist Christians *87*
Salvation by Paxil *88*
What the world really needed: another blogger *90*
A pagan again *94*
Some good news and bad news *101*

BOOK 2: Lessons from the Holy Wars

I. **LESSONS FROM THE DEPARTMENT OF HOMELAND INSECURITIES** *105*
Immigrants will catch the "America bug" without even realizing it *105*
Immigrants can re-teach Americans some personal discipline— but we should still draw the line at Shake 'n Bake *107*
A good devil can bring peace *108*
Soldiers, pirates, vampires and terrorists all have something in common *110*
Hawks fear "shrink"-age *112*
Most people's—and states'—attempts to become more secure seem to lead to their becoming less secure *115*
To understand Pakistani anti-Americanism, think of Pakistan as Washington's jilted lover *116*
When visiting Pakistan, expect no subtlety *118*
Arabs and South Asians would do well to stop "stomping on the ground" *121*

II. LESSONS FROM THE BICKERING GODS 123
A little psychology and a little Sufism can produce Islam 2.0 123
Moderates are lousy soldiers, so don't expect them to win holy wars or culture wars 125
Learn to be a disappointment 126
"True Believers" can dish it out but typically can't take it 127
It's more blessed to learn than to teach 128
After you fall out of love with Jesus, you can still be friends 132
The gods might give you a sign, but they hate you for asking 134
Christian faith is built on a powerful notion of sin and redemption... that few believe in the clutch 136
Strive to judge world events with intellectual consistency, even though your emotions won't cooperate 138
Life is ultimately about art, not about faith or fact 141
Dancing and religion aren't that different, and you can miss the joy in either 142
Gold's Gym and Thomas Aquinas don't have all the answers 143
Miracle pills are nice, but most of us have to live life the old-fashioned way—through hard work 145
Most people can't tolerate mystery 147
Evangelicals still have an opportunity to make a contribution through their beliefs 149

III. LESSONS FROM THE CLASH OF CULTURES 151
What racism? It's better not even to notice other's hostility 151
Clashes of civilizations are sometimes just sibling rivalries, taken too far 152
Immigrants should embrace their names, which can provide hours of amusement to others 154

A balanced view of world history is good for an immigrant's self-esteem 157

Sex, booze and bad traffic: You learn a lot about a society from the form of chaos it most dreads 158

Blondie's not so slutty after all. 159

On segregating the sexes: There are rooms, very exciting rooms, out there somewhere 160

The Bee Gees were evil, but you knew that 162

Hindus get the ladies. 164

Romance is the great struggle for Christian singles in the 21st century 165

Repress sex and it will eventually come out of your ears 168

A black comedy of Christian dating—or, how saving the world won't get you laid. 170

The patriarchs fear nothing more than a strong woman 173

Eat, drink, but don't be merry. 176

Oh, hell, just be merry. 177

Help others to shine, and you'll shine. 179

There is a place where we are all equal, though the sandwiches aren't cheap there 180

Epilogue: Dad Didn't Make It Back (And I Nearly Didn't Either) . . . 183

Acknowledgments 187

Foreword

What determines whether two people from different cultures will cooperate or spend their days plotting one another's demise?

In an age in which people from disparate backgrounds are more likely than ever to come into contact and into conflict, and an age in which such conflicts can be fought with more fatal force than ever, such issues increasingly will determine the fate of societies and of our planet.

It's for that reason that I believe we have much to learn from the experiences and insights of someone such as Rob Asghar, who has spent a lifetime exploring these issues in a deeply personal way. Asghar's immigrant family story is illuminating and encouraging – a hopeful sign that as each of us moves along our respective voyages of self-discovery and self-expression, even the most seemingly painful conflicts of identity and security can be overcome.

Such an insight may run counter to some of humanity's oldest impulses (a general preference for homogeneity of background or belief)—yet I believe it reflects an even deeper and greater impulse, one that a new generation of global citizens is equipped for: the desire to learn unceasingly, to become richer by understanding and appreciating what makes others different from us, and to give one another permission to grow in our own unique ways.

In my own studies and teaching, I've sensed that our younger generations are far more comfortable with a global context than the rest of us. They have traveled more than most of us, at younger ages, and are far more open to dissimilar vantage points. Many think of themselves as global citizens.

Asghar hit the mark when he wrote in the *Wall Street Journal* in 2002 that his personal narrative, involving culture clashes within his own family, intersected with a global narrative: In this book, he shrinks the so-called "clash of civilizations" to a family scale—mainly utilizing the backdrop of his own relationship with his immigrant father.

His anecdotes spell out both the cultural differences and similarities between his two homelands. He runs back to the Pan-American 747 as a four-year-old who glimpses exotic and chaotic Pakistan for the first time. As a teenager he witnesses attacks on the American embassy and his own American school in Islamabad, and later wonders if the Soviet invasion of Afghanistan might be a good opportunity for martyrdom, at the very moment that the U.S. breaks open a Pandoran jar of martyrs in the Af-Pak region. He frets, while in the U.S., about why his parents seem so much thriftier than the families of his free-spending American friends. He begins to drink more than his faith permits, which his father discovers the hard way. He leaves Islam for Jesus, devastating his family—then leaves Jesus too, shocking his Christian friends. He narrowly avoids being bombed by the Taliban in Islamabad, and amid the talk of a cosmic war between good and evil, he ponders why no one really takes seriously Jesus' admonition to "bless" our enemies.

Much of this book explores, in entertaining fashion, Asghar's relationship with his late father, Ali. Ali pursued an education in his rural, mud-hut village, despite his parents' demands that he stay home and work the family farm. Ali made it to the grand stage—America—and attempted to raise a family that would enjoy "the best of both worlds."

That was a fine sentiment not easily put into practice. As Asghar tilted away from Ali's values and his instructions, Ali recognized a Cats-in-the-Cradle recapitulation of the way he defied his own parents in order to follow his own dreams.

Ali returned to his Pakistani village late in life, to construct a school and hospital there, which improved access to quality education and healthcare for a thousand rural children—especially young girls who are forbidden such education by religious extremists. Whereas he once hoped to find the best of both worlds in America, he now spent his final years attempting to create it in a humble village which still lacked paved roads and had only minimal running water.

The stories in this book involve a fine fabric of troubles and triumphs. In my decades of studying how great leaders and institutions and even societies are forged, I have come to recognize that such forging happens most significantly in crucible moments within one's life. Trials transform us, and the searing heat of the crucible allows us to discover who we truly are.

The victories that Asghar discusses here, involving acceptance and reconciliation among people who can feel deserted and betrayed by their closest kindred, are victories, I think, for our larger family of human societies as they grind up against one another each day in an era characterized by identity politics and partisan posturing.

By sharing his journey of self-discovery across cultures and by revealing how one can hope both to be authentic and to be embraced for such authenticity, Asghar gives us hope that we can not merely survive but we can appreciate the differences of others. That is wonderful news for all of us.

Warren Bennis
Santa Monica, California

Introduction: "Who" Is Wise?

"*Ullu ka patha*!!!!" That was a common Urdu imprecation around most Pakistani and Pakistani-American households, including my own, when the parents were ticked off at the kids.

It translates literally as "son of an owl." That would strike many Westerners as a compliment, maybe even a self-serving one on the part of the parent. But its meaning is closer to "son of a bitch." It turns out that whereas an owl is the preeminent American icon of wisdom, the owl conveys an image of foolishness to a Pakistani.

I like how a Wikipedia entry for the phrase once noted, "Currently, this term is also used widely for the President of Pakistan (Asif Zardari) as a sign of great dislike by the people." When a struggling nation feels that way about its leader—as is usually the case in Pakistan—you can only brace yourself for what's coming next.

But how exactly does an American look at an owl and sense a professorial presence, while a Pakistani sees a frivolous rogue? How can one culture look at an image from nature and imbue it with one meaning while another culture imbues it with the opposite meaning?

Indeed, my decades at the peculiar intersection of Pakistani and American culture remind me in numerous ways that what one society finds to be sagacious will seem quite nitwitted to another. It's with this awareness that I offer these tales from the Pak-American intersection and these so-called lessons from the holy wars of our era, realizing that one person will find great folly precisely where another will find great insight.

And yet my chief hope is that the sum of the observations herein may help some to perceive their world through the eyes of another. And certainly that is where real wisdom resides.

BOOK 1

A Pakistani-American Odyssey

I: There Appears to Be Only One God, Allah, and Muhammad Is His Prophet

A match made in heaven and a mud-hut village

My father, Ali, met my mother, Parveen, at a wedding in Pakistan. It was their own wedding. As you may have surmised, this was an arranged marriage.

Much of that marriage, initiated nearly fifty years ago in a humble Third World country, would play out in the world's most advanced and alluring society. Pakistan was a sleepy country then, less than fifteen years removed from its independence from India. No one then expected Pakistan to capture the full attention of the West. No one expected the West's most powerful leaders and brightest minds to brood over it someday as an unprecedented global threat. Back then, no one could have known.

Dad was then a young man from the green, sugar-cane and cornfield farms of Pakistan, but his family managed to procure for him an elegant city girl as a bride. This is because, as one who'd begun a promising engineering career in the mystical and far-off land of America, he was something of a South-Asian Christopher Columbus. Thousands of people didn't fly back and forth between America and Pakistan every day the way they do today.

Father Knows Best?

Dad had been the youngest of seven brothers and sisters, and the most intellectually curious of the clan. When he was twelve, he loved school, but his father instructed him to drop out and work on the farm. He did so reluctantly. His elder brothers ordered him to stop moping, and he'd pen dark poems about how he'd someday exact revenge. Next, they'd find the poems and administer a suitable beating until he gave up on the idea of revenge. The cycle went on for some time. In the meantime, he'd find ways to sneak in whatever education he could get from textbooks and the like. He was a self-taught prodigy.

Pakistan is a place where you're supposed to do what your father says—especially back in that era, especially in a rural village free of outside temptations and influences. But Dad was persistent in wanting to prove himself in the classroom. His father finally relented and sent him back to school.

He excelled and went on to get a degree in engineering from a small Pakistani college. But he hadn't felt he'd proved himself yet, and he had an unusual amount of ambition and ample chutzpah. He and his brother Ramzan managed to obtain visas to study at North Carolina State University in 1956.

CULTURAL COLLISION 1: Brown man's burden

Dad was a man of medium height by the standards of his milieu, around 5'7", with relatively dark skin that he was slightly insecure about once he arrived in America, but he pushed past it.

Dad and Ramzan studied at N.C. State during segregation days, but they were category-busters. He later delighted in telling us about how he once went up to a "whites only" drinking fountain, then a "blacks only" drinking fountain, then announced loudly, "Well, they both taste the same." He said that bystanders chuckled.

He and Ramzan drove around the U.S. during the summer, saving money by working in pea canneries and tomato farms in places as far away as Oregon. Finding a good desk job or internship in the U.S. wasn't an option for Pakistani students then.

"I usually ended up finding ways to help the white owner improve his business," Dad would say, "and they would end up giving me a nice indoors job as a manager." Dad would then find ways to grab Cokes from the fridge and take them outside to his parched friends.

Upon earning his bachelor's degree in electrical engineering, Dad decided he would take a whack at getting an engineering job in America. His brother and friends laughed at him. Even Ph.D.s had to return to Pakistan or work at a car wash—how would he fare differently?

He worked the system a bit. He sweet-talked his way into being able to take IQ tests at prospective companies and would ace those tests. Companies then interviewed him based on the impression that he had a permanent work visa, and then the government gave him the visa based on the impression that he already had a job.

And so he caught on as the lone non-white person at the massive Western Electric headquarters in New York. For two weeks, he remained outwardly calm and inwardly petrified, sitting amidst a sea of white men sporting white shirts, light-colored ties and navy slacks. He dressed just as they did, but kept his coat on in an effort to out-professionalize them.

But he sometimes wondered if he should just walk away from the job and go work at the car wash that allowed some of his other U.S.-educated Pakistani friends to pay the bills.

After a few weeks, though, he once again proved his worth; he identified a more efficient way to do business and became a star around the offices. Dad's liability of being the odd brown person even became a distinguishing mark—he stood out.

All he needed now was a wife.

Saving sex, and handshakes, for marriage

Dad and Mom had seen pictures of one another and gotten general descriptions, but they never were allowed to speak or meet before their wedding. All details and negotiations were handled by their parents. Such arrangements prevented atrocities such as dating and romance.

Despite the lack of premarital contact, Dad did later boast, "I once rode past your mother's house on a motorcycle, and I was able to see her standing near the window." He was cheered by what he saw.

Mom was considered quite beautiful by both Pakistani and American standards. Dad was, well, in his words, "quite handsome enough, back when I had a full head of hair." For years after he lost his mop, he'd keep old pictures around to remind himself of former glories.

Pakistani wedding ceremonies and accompanied banquets linger endlessly, for four or more days, and the parents of the bride and groom may host dozens of relatives for weeks prior. A Pakistani marriage is a marathon compared to the American sprint, yet for some reason they both take about the same time and energy to produce.

When the pomp and circumstance and tedium ended for my mother and father, boy finally had a chance to meet girl. Dad and Mom began making each other's acquaintance in a, "It's very nice to meet you, let's go ahead and raise up this family" manner. Earnest Dad mentioned in passing that he's not much into "fun and games," and Mom thought, "Oh, great." But they became fast lifelong friends anyway.

A pregnant Mom rode on the back of my father's tiny motorcycle on long dirt-road treks back and forth between her city and his village. With no helmet. It was a different time, right? Then again, about the only thing that's changed is that some Pakistani cities today require the driver to wear a helmet, usually a loose-fitting, broken one, while his wife and kids ride side saddle on the back.

Ali & Harriet: the early days

Some months after their wedding, Dad returned stateside to continue in his new career. Mom, awaiting visa paperwork, delivered my older brother Shabi in Pakistan in mid-1962.

Shabi was the first of what Dad would call "my three tigers." Like your average firstborn, Shabi would have the sharpest teeth and best sense of the hunt. Mom brought the cub to the U.S. when he was just two months old, and baby and father gradually bonded. Shabi was the irrepressible one—all action, all passion, all the time. "The little son of a bitch has pepper up his ass," Dad once observed with dry detachment.

I came along three years later, the first and still the only family member born on American soil. This was in 1965, during our family's tenure in Sunnyvale, California, a period my parents would look back on as a Camelot experience for Pakistani immigrants. The people back in Pakistan envied us. We lived in a sparkling new $23,000 house in an immaculate pre-Silicon Valley neighborhood and drove a large Chevrolet. (I believe that house would cost about $1.5 million today, and for many years my parents fumed over their decision to sell it).

I was the quiet, mellow one. As a baby, Shabi awoke all ablaze, requiring immediate and constant attention. Yet when Shabi was not putting our parents through their paces or exclaiming loudly that he couldn't be expected to eat the gruel that my mother had prepared, he was skilled at impressing them and at winning the plaudits of his friends and American society. Straight As. National Honor Society. Class president. I, by contrast, kept my head in the clouds, thinking offbeat, non-linear thoughts that earned few high marks in school. I puzzled my parents; Pakistani culture is pragmatic, as many Third World societies are. Creative endeavors are a luxury only for people who have nothing left to achieve.

Mom was a quick and efficient homemaker, which left her long hours to watch soap operas and to draw up floor plans for the dream house in which we would all grow up—a house that could be the hub of the family's life for decades.

Dad spent long hours working at telecommunications firms to store up winter riches for the family while they watched their less long-haul-oriented American grasshopper neighbors squander their income on vacations, parties and fun, fun, fun. I suppose I appreciated that Mom and Dad were so opposed to the threat that would be posed in later years by parents such as Britney Spears, but I sometimes felt it wouldn't have killed them to let their hair down on occasion.

Less holy and more American than thou

Non-stop globetrotting should have minimized the Americanization of Shabi and me and increased our connection to our parents' home culture, but the reverse happened.

Because our parents placed us in American-operated schools while Dad was working in places such as Iran and Germany (and a British school in Uruguay), we were still immersed in Western culture.

Also, moving so often kept us from ever developing a set of long-term friends within a local Pakistani or Muslim community. There would be less "homeland peer pressure" or incentives to prod us to earn honor by memorizing more Quran verses than the next child. Less pressure to avoid thinking like white American kids.

My parents also set the stage for me to have a looser connection with their culture by not teaching us Punjabi, their native language, or Urdu, the slightly different Pakistani national language that served as an attempt to unify Pakistan's regions through one tongue that transcended regional dialects.

"I never wanted my children to be behind other children in any way," Dad told us years later. "I didn't care whether you learned Urdu, but I wanted you to speak perfect English so that you wouldn't be second-class in the classroom compared to the American children."

Modern linguists and Rosetta Stone salesmen now agree that kids can pick up multiple languages flawlessly, but I'm glad that Dad—using whatever knowledge was available at the time—was willing to err on the side of caution. Like many first-generation immigrants from other cultures, he placed our personal welfare ahead of his cultural obligations.

CULTURAL COLLISION 2: Hello, Pakistan, I hate you

Lots of people react with tears when they see their motherland for the first time. So did I, in a different way.

As a four-year-old, I gripped my parents' hands as we got off a plane that had delivered us to Karachi, the largest city in Pakistan. We entered the terminal, and I got my first glimpse of my ancestry's great Indus Valley civilization. It was like the cantina scene in Star Wars: A rowdy mob of people with long beards, headdresses, veils and other oddities were stomping around the terminal—everything but chickens, goats and horse carriages, which would be on the horizon soon enough.

I knew right away that something had gone wrong in our world:

White had become mocha, clean had become musty, cool had become humid, rosy had become, eh, aromatic.

I did what any sensible kid would do—I screamed and ran back into the airplane. Dad chase after me, scooped me up, and gradually introduced me to their land.

Six months later, having adjusted to brown people and the chickens, goats and scooters, along with the water buffalos, bicycles, beggars, bazaars, horse carts, horse droppings and other roadway delights, I allegedly remarked, "What happened to Brown Karachi?" My filter had changed quite a bit. That's a good thing about being a kid—you're a little more resilient than you are later in life.

Not many places in Pakistan seemed sanitary in the Western sense. We'd lived in the American Northeast a few times in my early life, in places such as Salem and Nashua in New Hampshire. Those places were quintessential American suburbia, a perfect blend of cleanliness and commercialism.

I'd inhale the fresh, gravelly fragrance of trampled parking-lot snow as we trudged into malls and shopping centers replete with new K-Marts and McDonald's and paradise-like grocery stores featuring every good substance known to our species. I would enjoy toasted pop-tarts while watching Kimba the White Lion on TV. America seemed like the perfect vending machine.

But on our too-frequent trips back to Pakistan, I'd be alarmed by the large, buzzing flies, the fragrances of zesty tandoori foods mingling with fresh street droppings from horses, the cows and chickens that moved like roving street gangs.

Love cannot be bought

We had more relatives than I could shake a stick at, and believe me, I tried shaking it to scare them off. Countless relatives, perhaps in the thousands or millions, no exaggeration: Api, our grandmother on Mom's side. Ummi, Mom's grandmother, who was the one who really brought Mom up. Lots of uncles and aunties. And hordes of male and female cousins like Imran, Zahid, Feri, Noshi and so on.

I did my best to communicate with my cousins, through broken Urdu and English. And, being kids, we were able to find enough games to play. The older adults were the most annoying. They insisted on loving, hugging, squeezing, kissing—something right out of a Journey song. They pinched cheeks till I was ready to cold-cock them in return.

Ummi, all 120 years and 55 pounds of her, once offered to give me cash in return for a kiss. I had my standards, so I shunned her wealth. As she grew infirm, the family locked her away at nights in a far corner room, where we could still hear her wailing at night due to her piercing migraines. It scared the nightlights out of me.

A mother of a motherland

Visits to Dad's village were also a chore, though more fascinating than a National Geographic Channel marathon. We made the pilgrimage several times during my own childhood. We drove for hours on country roads, surrounded by lush green fields through which green parrots swept in small flocks. Most parts of the village have lacked running water and power for most of the past 5,000 years. In the 1970s, local children were always startled to see us roll into town in one of those space-age contraptions known as automobiles—usually a Toyota Corona or another regal horseless carriage that could reach 60 mph with a running start. The kids would run alongside our car in excitement and thwack it with twigs. Cows and bulls and squawking chickens roamed the dirt paths. How very far from home. Except, as Dad reminded us, this somehow *was* home.

Get a job, you lazy quadriplegics

I was horrified by the sight of emaciated street people, sitting miserably on mats or on rolling boards that allowed them to just avoid the Grim Reaper while begging for spare change. I was alarmed by how common they were, and how nonchalant Pakistanis were about their presence. If I had any money on me, I'd try to give it to a beggar, only to be chided by a relative: "Don't give them any money! They aren't poor, they just beg for a living. Some of these people have cars at home."

"But, but...." I'd sputter. "That woman had no legs. How could she drive? And she only had one eye." I would hand a beggar some change when my uncles and aunts weren't looking.

Pakistan did have some charms, though, even for a child who preferred America. Its foods were tantalizing, especially its spicy barbecued goods and its lush, sweetly fragrant, golden mangoes and other tropical fruits. Desserts were another matter: Pakistanis have never been a subtle bunch, and their "mattai" sweets were heaping chunks of sugar, grease and foul spices.

Yep, once you grew used to the chaos of urban Pakistani life, you could hang out with your cousins and learn to enjoy places like the bazaars, those brightly decorated back-alleys that sold toys for children, fabrics for housewives, and cigarettes for men (and kids).

Twirling dervish

We traveled to Saudi Arabia for a trip to Mecca when I was five.

We woke early one still-dark morning and proceeded to make our way to the great temple, where my parents came to perform an Umrah. That is an unofficial pilgrimage to Mecca, but does not count as every able-bodied and able-walleted Muslim's need to perform a Hajj, or official pilgrimage.

It was still dark when my folks found an isolated spot at which to pray. And pray they did, as I hopped and skipped and twirled around the pillars of the temple, thinking, "This is fun—I'm playing in God's house." Mecca can inspire the loftiest thoughts about the grandeur of the Divine, as well as a sense of communal intimacy. The pillars, arches, domes and golden calligraphy are a transfixing experience.

We later orbited with a sea of white-clad humans around the Ka'aba, the little black-cloth-covered cubical building that Muslims believe was built by Abraham. Once we got all the way to the Ka'aba, my father instructed me to kiss a smoothened rock attached to the outside.

Even at a young age, a little hypochondria set in. Everybody else had been kissing it. What about germs? I realized that an all-powerful God was supposed to take care of that and gave it a quick peck. The holy rock was tied in legend to Abraham, although the less reverent consider it a meteorite.

I felt quite aware of a majestic, holy God throughout my childhood. He was on my mind almost constantly, although girls seemed to be on my mind at an early age too. This I remember from my keen attraction to the secretary in Sad Sack comics that I read at the age of five or six. (I often called upon this memory later when my many implosions on the launching pad of romance made me wonder if I might be gay). Often, such childhood thoughts about cartoon secretaries led to guilty shivering before God.

A little slice of America called Tehran

We moved to Tehran, Iran in 1973, when I was in third grade so that Dad could take a job there with a branch of Northrop. The Shah was firmly in power, and we joked about his secret police overhearing any criticism we might make of his regime. At the same time, I was impressed by Iranian society's progressiveness. It seemed far more advanced, in the consumerist Western sense, than Tel Aviv would seem some thirty years later. Women walked the streets in skirts, shopping centers sold Americanesque lifestyles, and fundamentalists quietly fumed that things were getting out of hand and that there'd be a reckoning someday. They reckoned, all right.

The Fonz Cometh

My younger brother Ferhan arrived in Tehran in 1974, moving me from youngest child to middle child in one swoop nine years after my own birth. His birthplace later prompted me to briefly call him "The Little Ayatollah" in a wrong-headed jab at the devout Muslim faith he'd later display.

Ferhan was the spunky and bright object of the entire family's affection. Shabi became a second father to him, bringing him up in his own image, teaching a toddling Ferhan to give a thumbs up and say "Ayyyy!!!" like Fonzie. Maybe Ferhan would be the family's all-American.

Dad loved having "three tigers." He and Mom spent their evenings thinking out loud in front of us tigers about their vision for the future, which centered on our becoming doctors. And living together on the same street. And being one eternally closely-knit bunch. With good Pakistani wives, not the slutty American kind. We spent many evenings together in the master bedroom, dreaming how our lives would be, as Mom and Dad reclined and enjoyed their brood. Shabi and I would argue about whether we would all have red cars or green cars. I imagined massive Ford LTDs.

CULTURAL COLLISION 3:
Religious cartoons, without the rioting

Our nomaderie continued when Northrop moved us to northern Virginia in 1974. There, Mom and Dad worked hard to prevent us from being exposed to negative influences—especially Christianity. A Christian tract, in the form of a comic-strip morality play, made its way into our mailbox one day; and for reasons I still do not understand, they kept the tract—but they stapled together the offensive pages, and placed it above the refrigerator.

Any artistic depiction of God is offensive to Muslims, just as it is to most Jews. And many of this tract's pages dealt with scenes in which a debauching sinner dies suddenly and is transported to the throne of God in Heaven, who sits in somber judgment. Dad or Mom had stapled those pages together because they illustrated God, albeit in a vague, faceless manner.

I was naturally curious, especially about things I wasn't supposed to know about, so I managed to peek between the stapled pages. Some of the stapled pages at the end talked about how Jesus was the offspring of God, which seemed far-fetched and weird. However, I was fascinated to gaze at the image of a majestic, eerie and faceless God on a throne. I felt naughty and frightened for having done so, but did it anyway. It was like a pornographic thrill.

When a Charlie Brown Christmas looks relatively impressive

As a sixth grade student at Hunt Valley Elementary School in Springfield, Virginia, I received a particularly vexing homework assignment in early December. My challenge: to bring an ornament to add to the Christmas tree that our teacher had brought to class.

Granted, every other student had received the same assignment, but it was a challenge for me. What does a cool Christmas ornament look like? Where does one go to purchase a Christmas ornament that would not be laughed at? Would bringing certain kinds of ornaments be too traditional or too sissy or too whatever? Where does one even go to buy one of these things?

I brought the problem home to my mom and dad, who were empathetic. They were not horrified to have a Christian holiday thrust upon them. As far as they and I could tell, Christmas was about celebrating the birthday of Jesus, and given that he was a prophet in great standing within Islam, they saw no problem with his special day. They occasionally even gave us presents in honor of the occasion, and during some Decembers we really lived large, bringing home a two-foot tall potted pine tree.

But those trees were pre-decorated. Now we had to go find a suitable ornament for a public tree. Dad drove me to the nearby Hechinger's hardware store after dinner one evening, and we wandered around, looking at their Christmas displays. He and I settled on a small, plastic, felt-covered Santa object. After paying the $1.39 for it, we were done. I think Dad was less flummoxed than I by the whole process, but I found it all quite taxing. When you're a nerd, and only a semi-American nerd at that, you begin to put too much thought into everything.

Shabi and I both wondered if we would have had a grand advantage if our parents had understood American ritual—holiday dinners, vacations, dating protocol—as well as other parents. It took us years to find that our American peers had their own foibles and traumas while attempting to fit in.

I did rather enjoy the Christmas season and envied Americans who were able to stage the entire spectacle each year. It wasn't as if I cared about whether Jesus was the reason for the season, I simply found the bright lights, the festive colors and the commercialism to be the living symbol of the Rockwellian America that I craved.

Can't judge a book by its unintelligent cover

I have a long history of exceeding other people's low expectations. After college graduation, a professor wrote me a recommendation letter urging prospective employers "not to underestimate Rob... he is more intelligent and perceptive than he may seem at first."

Yet sixth grade was also when I showed my first signs of being brighter than I looked, as I churned out a few good science reports on red blood cells and the like. At an awards assembly, the teachers called me up to present me with an achievement award in science. In an amazing coincidence, my mother and father were in the front row of the assembly—Dad had somehow gotten off work to be there!

Mom later told me that they had actually received advance notice that I would be getting the award, and it struck me as quite nice that they would want to attend my big moment. I now knew how overachieving Shabi must have felt on his regular jaunts up our school auditorium's aisle to pick up some new prize.

And yet not even my science award could save me when I entered seventh grade and a new school a few miles down the road. Unlike elementary school, middle school heavily revolved around compartments called "lockers," complete with Byzantine devices called combination locks. Though our teachers drilled into us the "right, left, left" procedure for opening them, I somehow wasn't getting it. Academic awards be damned; I proved myself an idiot yet again. I lugged seven classes worth of books home, and cried on my Dad's shoulder, dimly aware that I was at least crying privately for a change instead of in full public view, where I usually cried. It was progress.

Alex Haley only appreciated his roots because he didn't have to live there

Our 747 touched the sun-scorched earth of Pakistan in September of 1978. I reacted on the outside with a bit more dignity than the four-year-old who ran back into the airplane cabin, but I was much the same person on the inside.

Transplanted again from the fragrant, manicured consumerist perfection of American suburbia into the funk of Pakistan, I experienced withdrawal symptoms. A life without McDonald's and its quick burger fix. A life without milk that tasted cool and fresh, as opposed to Pakistan's greasy, gamey milk that tasted as though it had udder bits floating at the bottom of the glass. A life without grocery stores lined with rows of pop-tarts and other staples. Without central heat or air conditioning that could be counted on to work all day. Without being driven around in cool, big cars.

Instead, we had to get used to life in a Third World country. With buses that poured out mammoth clouds of choking exhaust, and cars that sped through alleys, over sidewalks, or wherever else they pleased. With beggars lining the streets. With that odd mélange of smells in the marketplace. And, granted, with many charms as well.

Islamabad was a planned capital city, positioned at the feet of the lush and majestic Margalla Hill range. Much of it was notably tidier than your typical Pakistani hamlet. And Pakistan's grilled meats were rich, spicy and pungent, and its fruits were sweeter than most anything you could get in the States, even though the American versions were artificially "enhanced."

Feeling "trapped" in this young, clean and green city, I craved suburban American consumerist trappings, and I found myself fantasizing that I could get back to the U.S. just for a weekend to run through a good grocery store or shopping mall.

Islamabad's grocery and pharmacy stores were tiny and cramped. Fresh foods were sold in outdoor markets teeming with flies. Pharmacies had a distinct medicinal smell that nauseated me. No fancy shampoo to be found, just an odd-smelling, locally-bottled "egg shampoo," which covered your head like an egg yoke grasping for its life. Colas tasted a bit peculiar there. Pop-tarts? None to be found. And forget Big Macs and those greasy fries. Pakistan had approximations of most American things, and those approximations seemed to be mockeries.

Over time, I did scrape up an ability to embrace some aspects of Pakistan that the U.S. couldn't touch, especially those ridiculously sweet mangos, the spicy kabobs sold on streets and in restaurants, and those wonderfully crisp and savory veggies that you only find in Chinese restaurant dishes in that part of the world.

Be true to your high-security, diplomatic enclave school

Mom and Dad enrolled Shabi and me in Islamabad's American-run school, the International School of Islamabad, a cozy K-12 school of about 400 students, which seemed about 60% American, 10% Pakistani and 30% Foreign Service brats from Britain, Argentina, France, Australia, Yugoslavia and other foreign countries. The vast majority of American students there worked for either the embassy or the U.S. Agency for International Development. The remainder may have had parents in oil or other industries.

Mom enrolled Ferhan in the mostly English-speaking Froebel School, a much less costly Pakistani-run school, since his young age made him more adaptable and less likely to protest. This meant he would learn the Quran and speak Urdu and Punjabi, whereas Shabi and I would study Western history and speak French.

Shabi and I had to prove our mettle to our American peers at ISI (the school is now known as ISOI because ISI now more famously refers to Pakistan's version of the CIA, the Inter-Services Intelligence.

American students there expected us to be more like the local, thick-accented indigenous Pakistanis whom they caricatured behind their backs. Soon, after talking to us, the Americans would note, "Geez, you're just like an American." Yeah we were.

We made our new setting into as much of a home as possible, and we began to make friends with many of the American students but few of the Pakistanis and other international students.

Sweeping poverty under the rug

"This place is awful," I whined to my mother. "At least the American diplomat kids at school get to go to a commissary. Do you know they have Ding-Dongs and Twinkies there?"

"Well, I find that Americans here are very open-minded. I see their women dressed in Pakistani clothes in public. You could try wearing some Pakistani clothes for a change. Americans are very adventurous. Not like you."

She was right. Open-minded adult Americans, the kind who freely signed up for Foreign Service because they found lesser civilizations to be charming, considered Pakistan to be a cultural delight. They were the kinds of people who actually read *National Geographic* instead of leaving it on the coffee table.

Truthfully, I wouldn't have been much happier in France or many other first-world nations that had far more squalor than did Springfield or Nashua. I probably would have hated many parts of Los Angeles or New York. I was specifically a fan of American suburban life.

My American peers in Islamabad were divided as to whether they preferred to live stateside or in Third World settings. They lived like royalty in Islamabad. Whereas the typical upper-middle-class Pakistani family had two or three housekeepers and cooks, the Americans often had five or more. The American kids could demand a cup of tea from a servant, whereas their mother would snap at them if they attempted to get her to do their bidding while in the States.

The American embassy paid the servants for its diplomatic families far better than Pakistani families paid their servants, and the former were far better groomed.

I was always struck by how awful the life of a servant was, and how the upper classes didn't feel any guilt over paying a floor sweeper a few dollars a day. The servants would return at night to a mud-hut village outside Islamabad. Oftentimes, a cook would stay in small quarters behind our house, going home only on weekends to see his wife and children.

It seemed a fundamentally flawed system. As long as they were paid so little money, what hope did they have for a better future? On the other hand, what self-respecting middle-class Pakistani person would pass up the chance to have such servants doing all the dirty work?

I was also puzzled by the habit of haggling in Pakistani bazaars. Upper-middle-class housewives would berate eight-year-olds tending the family fruit stand as a bargaining ploy, then would have their driver carry a sack of mangoes obtained through such shrewd negotiation. But the transaction only left the kid in poverty and the woman's family in relative comfort. It seemed part of a larger, dysfunctional system that was destined to fail.

The sweepers were an especially sad lot. Pakistani brooms consisted of a bunch of thin, two-foot long twigs. Because Pakistan had yet to invent the broom handle, the sweepers had to squat and move back and forth around the floor like crabs. They became so sadly efficient at that sort of movement and posture that they took tea breaks in that fashion.

I wanted to buy them all broom handles, and I would ask my mother why no one at least imported the good American kind if no one was able to generate the technology indigenously. Again, it reminded me of chopsticks: Sure, they were a handy eating method for Asians for thousands of years; but once they saw forks, they should have said, "Okay, let's retire these little sticks." Instead, the *National Geographic* crowd of Americans insisted on learning how to use them and to claim that Chinese food tasted better that way.

• • • • • • •

In my English class during my first year at ISI, I discovered that I had some moxie, despite my great shyness.

We were assigned a speech on a topic of our choosing, and I decided to talk about how Islam was the one true religion. My classmates, who were mostly Christian, peppered me with tough questions and rebuttals, but I held my ground. I do not suppose anyone converted to my way of thinking, although I used to pray that such a thing might happen.

Shabi, a junior, tried out and made the school basketball team, which participated in an annual tournament of American schools from Pakistan, Afghanistan and India. Skinny then (but stocky now), he was a backup guard who seemed slightly timid on the court—the only time I'd ever known my hard-charging hero to be so deferential. He worked on his game, though, and fully expected to be a starter and a star his senior year.

I had lesser goals, like not getting laughed at. During square dancing in gym class, I noticed the pretty and petite and snobby Jennifer, everyone's first crush, groaning and making noises to a nearby friend as she and I were rotating into position to dance with one another. That friend happened to be the equally snobby Ayesha Khan. Ayesha was the privileged daughter of AQ Khan, who also fathered Pakistan's atomic bomb program and its bomb-selling program. So I had the honor of being laughed at by the bomb-maker's daughter, though at the time I only knew that her father was rich, not that he was an international menace.

CULTURAL COLLISION 4: Rob meets Bizarro Rob

A tall, thin, serious-countenanced Pakistani student showed up at our Islamabad school early in ninth grade. His name was Altaf. He spoke fluent English, which fascinated me and made me somewhat jealous about protecting my territory as the only Westernized Pakistani in my class.

Altaf and his family would end up being Bizarro versions of my family and me. Altaf hailed from Toronto, Canada. Or, more accurately, his family was from Pakistan, moved to Canada, then decided after about two decades that it was time to return to their true home. Altaf, his older sister Amera and younger brother Jasim were the advance team in this move, renting a house and enrolling in our school.

Altaf swiftly made enemies with the white Americans at our school because he was wildly opinionated about many topics, especially on the vast superiority of Canada to the U.S. He would drive Americans to fits, me included, with constant sniffs about how Canada was more advanced, more civilized, more fragrant, more everything. He often came close to a caning.

But he came in fact not to praise Canada but to bury it. He and Amera, then 17, were convinced they could never be Canadians and that their salvation lay in reclaiming their Pakistani identity. They were there to stay.

Oh, and by the way, they knew that I should do the same. Altaf and Amera were filibustering Terminators in their ability to stay on their point and knock me from my own point.

"Look," Altaf would say. "You're kidding yourself. You'll never be accepted fully there."

"I already am. I get along just fine with everyone. They accept me and they accept all kinds of people."

"No, you're wrong. You think they accept you but they really don't."

"Look, you're full of it. But even if what you said was true, this country isn't home for me either."

His sister would jump in. "Yes it is. You just have to give it a chance. Learn the customs and the reasons for them. Try to appreciate it. You're just running from yourself."

"I'm not running from anything! Leave me the hell alone!"

Oddly, though religious in their zeal for their homeland, neither of them was particularly orthodox about Muslim faith, nor was anyone else in their family. Islam was not the force that drove them home. It was something else—a purely cultural longing, a sense that their skin color and background would keep them from ever finding the place they longed for within Canada's social hierarchy.

**CULTURAL COLLISION 5: "Death to America,"
the popular new game everyone's playing**

That fall, the school hired a new principal, who used to be at Tehran American School, another school that Shabi and I had attended a few years earlier. Because of political problems in Tehran, most Americans were sent back stateside and the school shut down. The principal came to Islamabad—then in a truly sad twist of fate, decided to return to Tehran to have some of that school's books shipped over to us. He ended up being one of the 52 hostages that spent some 400 days trapped there.

He was not the only one who had a rotten autumn.

On the afternoon of November 21, 1979, we students were escorted to the auditorium to watch movies at a time when we would normally be catching our school buses for the ride home. After the umpteenth screening of whatever they could dredge up, more and more of us were wondering aloud why we were there. The answer came back through a relay of whispers: local citizens were attacking the U.S. embassy on the other edge of town. A rage of anti-Americanism had suddenly swept the streets. It seemed so surprising at the time, so unexpected. School administrators decided wisely that they did not want us to go home in school buses that would have signaled that we were Americans. They instead began calling parents at home to ask them to pick us up.

A certain amount of fear spread throughout the auditorium. Might we be attacked? The answer came a few hours after the sequestering, when school officials suddenly commanded us to move to the gymnasium area.

While a long procession of us was doing so, we suddenly heard shouts and the crash of glass breaking. A number of us raced into a locker room, which someone bolted shut. Little girls shrieked and sobbed, while most everyone trembled with dread about what would come next.

Not I. I was in some kind of mysterious zone. I thought this was the wildest, most exciting thing that had ever happened in my life, not counting the kindergarten kids who bashed my head into the wall during my time attending a British school in Uruguay.

So while others wailed, I stood wide-eyed and smiling. Maybe I was trying to show how tough I was, or maybe I was trying to model calm. Shabi grabbed me: "You jerk! Stop smiling! These girls are scared to death. People will kill you if they see you acting like that!"

The smile evaporated.

Soon we were let out of our locker room by school staff who told us the coast was clear. It turned out to be only a small remnant of protesters that made it to our school. And after breaking a few windows and scaring the pants off my classmates, the last violent stragglers cooled down and were chased off by groundskeepers wielding rakes.

Soon Mom arrived, with her driver, to take us home. We learned more facts. The angry mobs were fueled by a false rumor of an American invasion of the Saudi holy city of Mecca. That day a band of Muslim radicals momentarily took control of the temple there, which hosts millions of pilgrims each year from around the world—but someone conveniently started the rumor that Americans did it. This "news" raged across Islamabad that morning, and public buses and private cabs began giving free rides to the American embassy, so long as the riders agreed to help burn the place down.

They ravaged the sprawling, multi-million dollar embassy compound that I considered to be a shrine on my few visits there. I cherished it because it offered a rare opportunity to feel once again like I was "home." They also killed two American workers, including a Marine. Thousands of ordinary Joes and Jilals became one-day terrorists because of a bad rumor about American desecration of the Muslim holy land.

The next day, the State Department sent out its orders: evacuate all diplomatic families, except a few essential staff. I lost all my friends again.

Shabi and his dream of starring on the basketball team? Those dreams were ground to dust. He and the entire senior class were granted an anticlimactic graduation six months ahead of schedule, and he returned to the U.S. to sulk and to work at McDonald's.

On November 27, 2004, just twenty-five years after the attacks, the *Washington Post* would go on to examine that day, noting that in hindsight it should have been a harbinger of things to come. From an article titled, "A Day of Terror Recalled: 1979 Embassy Siege in Islamabad Still Haunts Survivors:"

> Twenty-five years later, this outburst seems a thin slice of history, sandwiched between the taking of U.S. hostages in Iran and the Soviet invasion of Afghanistan. Officially, Nov. 21 was quickly forgotten, seen by the United States as an aberration in its complex but generally productive relationship with Pakistan.
>
> For many of the people who endured the embassy attack and its aftermath, these events linger, called to mind each year as Thanksgiving approaches.

One of my classmates, the red-headed, loudmouthed Adam Rice, was quoted in the story:

> Some who endured the attacks on the embassy and the school later concluded that the lack of a U.S. reaction made the United States look weak. Adam Rice, who as a ninth-grader broke his wrist fleeing protesters at the school, says the lesson of Iran and Pakistan was that those hostile to Americans "can stick them in the eye, and they don't do anything back."

He joined the Army after high school and served in Afghanistan in 2002 as a Special Forces reservist, contributing to a strengthened U.S. posture in the face of attack.

It was not at all surprising to read that Rice had gone in that direction. He always seemed like a "God and guns made America great" kind of guy. But I was reunited with him three decades later on Facebook. Funny world.

A pawn of the bomb-maker's daughter

Classes for the rest of us resumed a few weeks later, but my ninth-grade class shrank from 30 people to 12. And I couldn't stand most of those twelve. I moped a good deal and took long walks, and wondered what was happening to our world.

I ran for class president against Ayesha, the snobby daughter of the bomb-maker, and somehow managed to lose even though most of my peers claimed they'd voted for me. Either they lied or the teacher who counted the votes lied, but either way I felt robbed of a minor pride.

I also found that the remaining students at our school changed drastically once the Americans left. The Pakistanis, Yugoslavians and Germans suddenly rose up and assumed roles as big men and women on campus, whereas they were subservient to the Americans before. They clearly relished having their time in the limelight. I loathed them. And I missed America.

Altaf of Canada, his sister Amera and brother Jasim attempted to make Pakistan their permanent home, succeeding in fits and spurts and managing to learn the language and make some local friendships. Their parents arrived at long last, and things deteriorated in terms of my own peace of mind.

Their father was a beast. The apple indeed doesn't fall far from the tree—Altaf and Amera were callow apprentices of a blustery maestro of browbeating. Their father was a headstrong rural man, a very intelligent debater.

"Robbie, you are a complete fool to think you have a home in America," he would say in a manner that could trigger weeks of insomnia. "Do you really think you can grow up and be a true success there?"

"Sure. Absolutely."

"No. Here is where you are wrong. They may like you, but they do not want you marrying their daughters. They may like you as a neighbor, but they do not want you in the family. There are limits to the life you can live there. Here, there are no limits to the kind of life you can have."

"No, I think there are limits here to who I can be. I'm willing to take my chances there, sir. I just think you're exaggerating how bad it is."

These tormentors stayed on me, offering daily blasts of their evangelical zeal. I often wished we could disengage, but it became harder after Mom befriended Altaf's mother and Ferhan befriended Jasim.

The family's voices haunted me. As annoying as they were, as over-opinionated as they were, they were hardly fools; rather, they were astute, perceptive people. Were the odds of making it in America longer than I had realized?

What made it more complicated was that, as I had indicated to them, Pakistan did not feel like home for me. I liked Big America, with all its opportunities, all its conveniences, and all its consumerism. I loved the openness and the efficiency of that culture, and reviled the inefficiency and insular quality of Pakistan.

In America, perhaps I would not be totally accepted, but I would be free. Free to make choices and live out those choices. Free to enjoy a range of experiences. Free to be stimulated by countless forms of ideas. That mattered. Color TV and Twinkies were just bonuses.

Years later, Eric Hoffer's *True Believer* helped make sense of many forms of human silliness, including the kind that Altaf's family suffered from. We proselytize, Hoffer wrote, because our considerable self-doubt spurs us to drown our doubts in the company of others and in the unanimity of shared convictions. That can cause some good things, but also many bad things. Altaf and Amera needed to convert me to their point of view. Their own confidence in their choice was not sufficient to keep them going; they needed to know that their choice was so utterly proper that any sane person in their shoes would make it.

Rambling on

The highlight of my remaining time in Islamabad was when I found the courage to make a cold call on a rare American man still in town. Mr. Coffield was the father of Shabi's best friend, and although he had sent his son Eric back to the States, Eric's stash of Led Zeppelin albums remained behind. Shabi had tried to turn me on to Led Zeppelin, but I'd listened to Robert Plant's yowling and dismissed them as demented perverts. Still, I thought the music was sort of seductive.

Later, though, I'd check out the articles and the swaggering Zeppelin concert pictures I would see on the *Hit Parader* magazines that I would find at an Islamabad bookstore. They seemed so... godlike, so larger than life. I read more and learned more about their seminal role in rock and came to be fascinated by their mystique.

So I spent large amounts of time summoning the moxie to knock on Mr. Coffield's door. He was happier to let me in than I'd expected. I made small talk, then I got to the point. I wanted to borrow his son's records. He showed me to Eric's record collection, and I stood in hushed amazement, like the person who discovered King Tut. I brought the precious records home, taped them with loving care on the family tape/phonograph stereo, and became a lifelong Zeppelin fan. They would be the band that got me through high school, through college, and through life, even though my friends and peers usually mocked me in the 1980s before they became a legend to newer generations. I would later love Mozart, Oscar

Peterson and Bach—but there was only one Zeppelin, even though Shabi no longer cared for them.

CULTURAL COLLISION 6: The coming of the godless communists, and the beginning of the end of the Pakistan we once knew

Christmas in Pakistan is no huge deal. Muslims agree with Christians that Jesus was born of a virgin and became a great messiah. But there is no inclination to Christmas trees and gift-giving. So when I woke up the day after Christmas in 1979, it seemed an ordinary enough morning. Then I heard the news reports that Soviet troops had stormed into Afghanistan's capital, Kabul.

The world quaked during one of the most jarring moments of the Cold War. The Russians were making a beeline to the Persian Gulf. With Afghanistan now conquered, only Pakistan stood in its way. Islamabad was a mere 230 miles from Kabul.

It was the first time in my life that backward, anonymous Pakistan became an interesting country. Washington stepped up its support for Islamabad, because Pakistan was a crucial domino that the U.S. could not afford to let fall. From Pakistan, Washington equipped and dispatched freedom fighters (men such as Osama bin Laden, who would later symbolize the law of unintended consequences).

Would Soviet tanks next steamroll into Islamabad? It seemed a possibility.

• • • • • • •

I continued to make the best of Islamabad as my home, taking long, solitary walks in 100-degree sun and 80% humidity to which I'd become accustomed. Mom knew I was miserable, so she offered me a healthy allowance that allowed me to eat my way to happiness. I found excellent tandoori food at local restaurants and even some excellent English-trifle-like desserts with heapings of cake, pudding and fruit.

It was hard to fast in the U.S., when no one around me was fasting save my family. But in Islamabad during the summer (when school was not in session), I managed to fast an entire Ramadan month—and gained ten pounds. Bear in mind that you only need to fast from sunset to sundown, which leaves all kinds of early morning and late night opportunities to gorge, with ample time to hibernate like a bear.

Islamabad was a sleepy town, but during Ramadan, people lined the streets at night and stores and restaurants stayed open late as everyone celebrated the end of the fast. The next day, most restaurants would be closed until the next sundown.

California Dreaming

The U.S. government had begun dispatching Foreign Service families back to Islamabad late in the summer of 1980—a mix of old and new families. I looked forward to being a seasoned veteran at our Islamabad school. Our school had even opened a teen center not far from where I lived, where we could listen to (relatively) new rock records, play air hockey, and enjoy orange Fanta drinks and brownies. I was finally getting comfortable in a place I had hated for so long.

And just then, our time in Pakistan grinded to a halt in September of 1980. Mom and Dad had run out of money to fund their construction activities in Islamabad, so Mom, Ferhan and I boarded a plane to rejoin Shabi and Dad in…. California.

California…. The name caused a ripple in my heart. I had heard about it and read about it—and had been mesmerized. I had kept in Islamabad a KLM flight magazine that Dad brought to us on a visit, an issue that spotlighted California in all its glory.

There could not possibly be a more magical place on earth, or a more "American" place. Palm trees, sunshine, Disneyland. It was to America what America was to the rest of the world. I was dizzy at the prospect of going there.

Sure, I'd been born there, but we had moved shortly thereafter. This was a peculiar homecoming to a place that seemed so beyond a small-time pseudo-American like me.

Party like a verb

My family and I sought to settle into Thousand Oaks, a cheery and pleasant Southern California bedroom community, just an hour north of L.A.'s hive of smog, traffic and palm trees. It was something of a challenge for me and Ferhan to adjust to America again.

Ferhan had been born in Tehran as an American citizen, but spent almost all of his first four years in the U.S. He was an all-American kid, before we spent the next two years in Islamabad. Now he was back in the U.S., his identity a bit more murky.

Shabi, meanwhile, was torn about whether he should go to college back east, where he had a few opportunities, or follow us to California. Family and California had more allure, and he joined us.

Thousand Oaks in the first two years of the 1980s was for all intents and purposes a real-world version of *Fast Times at Ridgemont High*, with surfing Jeff Spicolis, partying dudes and cute blondes who looked like Heather Locklear (who actually attended my high school about three years before I did, as did Belinda Carlisle of the Go-Go's).

This was the first time that I heard "party" used as a verb. I imagined lots of pointy hats and noisemakers every Friday night, but began to realize that it mainly involved alcohol, music and standing around. "That's a party?" I wondered to myself.

I still gave fitting in my best shot. I bought bright and sunny surfer-style t-shirts and "boot-cut" jeans from Miller's Outpost (now known as Anchor Blue). I then discovered, to my irritation, that the bell-bottom look was out. Pray tell, why then did they sell those jeans anymore? I still feel betrayed decades years later.

Yet I plodded onward, getting my hair layered in the feathery manner of the times. Contact lenses helped complete the overhaul.

The legend had it that girls were more beautiful and more blonde in California. I found many of them to be stunning, but determined that much of the hubbub and songs about California girls were hype, just like with Italian girls who are less attractive on balance than British women.

· · · · · · ·

Family life in Thousand Oaks seemed even more confusing than when I was younger, as it should be for any teenager. But this was compounded for me by my needing to navigate the California culture gaps in addition to the generation gap with my parents.

Still, there was amusement to be had there. Years before "Crossfire" or "The McLaughlin Group," before "The Jerry Springer Show" or MTV's "Real World," Dad and Shabi could have drawn large audiences with their verbal jousting. Dad had been born correct on a vast number of issues, as far as he could tell. As far as Shabi could tell, he had been born to correct Dad, who usually didn't appreciate the intervention.

They sparred about matters small and large, over trivial facts or world issues. On family outings we often could not get to the first red light without Dad telling Shabi in no uncertain terms to keep his big mouth shut, which would result in thirty minutes of silence before the tension broke.

In one argument, Dad pointed out his considerable edge in life experience over Shabi, saying, "I know much more than you about anything." Shabi would feel compelled to throw out a trivia question about the average rainfall in Brazil, prompting a rebuke, which then prompted Shabi to go to his room and slam the door.

Dad could never tolerate the tension for long, however, especially if anyone in the house considered him the source of the tension.

A knock on the door would come. "Come on, Shabi, come out," Dad would say.

"No."

"Please, come on, Shabi. Let's not be mad."

"Dammit, Dad, I am mad."

"Oh, come on, Shabi. Come on out."

This went on for several minutes, at which point Shabi would emerge from his room, Dad would give him a bear hug and tell him not to argue with him anymore, and the family would go on about its business.

CULTURAL COLLISION 7: Is there a *real* doctor in the house?

Pakistanis believe there is only one profession in the world that is both noble and profitable: doctor. And by that, we mean a real doctor. Medical doctor.

Dad loved to tell the story of how his brother-in-law was once on an airplane when the stewardess came up to him and said, "Excuse me; I couldn't help but notice on the passenger list that you're a doctor. We need your help with one of our other passengers."

His brother-in-law responded, "Oh, actually, I'm a Ph.D. in psychology."

The stewardess said "Oh, terrific. Never mind."

In other words, in the prestige sweepstakes, only MDs need apply. However, if one cannot become a physician, a child should at least aspire to become an engineer or a civil servant. Artists, writers and poets are reprobates.

Shabi, the family star who had been thoroughly infected by Americanization, did not care about being a doctor anymore. He was all entrepreneur. He took a job stocking shelves at a drug store, which kept Mom and Dad awake at night, and majored in business at a college they had never heard of: Cal State Northridge or Cal State Nothing or Cal State No Privilege or something to that effect.

Meanwhile, I became a writer for the school newspaper, the *Newbury Park Prowler*. I first was rattled by the idea of having my writing seen by intelligent people, or even by the students at my school. I only ended up in the class because my counselor asked me what my interests were, and I responded "communications" (meaning telecommunications and engineering). He said, "Oh, journalism is communications, so let's put you on the school paper," and I was too shy to say he was crazy and that I'd never put my writings out in public view, where they could be ridiculed.

Mentored by our journalism teacher, Karin Levine, I survived my shyness and even grew to love the notoriety. I wrote album reviews in which I roundly denounced every rock performer as inferior to Led Zeppelin. This made me quite unpopular with some people, especially once '70s rock fell out of fashion immediately after my junior year. Dad loved reading my pieces and gave me $10 for every article that I got published.

I later ventured into geo-politics in my editorials, criticizing Israeli policies, which I believed were unfair to Palestinian Muslims. That got me sent down to the school office be lectured by a school staffer—a concentration camp survivor who felt I'd wronged Israel. I then wrote a puff piece on her to make amends, and wouldn't write about Israel again in high school; in later years, I continued to criticize Israeli policies, but learned a lesson about sensitivity regarding people who treat the issue as a personal matter of life and death. I also realized Israel was often a third-rail issue: Don't touch it if you don't have to.

Loving life on *The Prowler*, I decided during my junior year that I was meant to be a writer, not a doctor or engineer. Mom was not delighted. "Look what you've done with your stupid $10!" she would bellow at Dad. "You're turning him into an idiot!"

Dad was more measured and logical about the whole affair. One day, as we sat in our parked Buick LeSabre together while Mom shopped for fabric and Ferhan ran off to buy a donut, Dad looked at me and said, "I've made a decision. You will be a doctor. I have thought about this and I have made my decision. No discussion. You will be a doctor."

Annoyed beyond words, I just sat there. His edict precluded debate. Would I run away from home? I did not know if I could scrape up any intention of obeying him. After all, he did not listen to his demanding father when Grandpa ordered him to give up getting the education he wanted.

I later argued the point with him at our house. "How can I become interested in something I just don't like?" I asked.

"You can begin to like it if you give it a chance."

"No, I can't. Some things you just can't learn to love. Here, let me prove it to you. I'm going to play a record by my favorite band. I can assure you that no amount of listening to it will help you to like it."

I put Led Zeppelin II on the turntable, turned up the volume, and blasted out "Whole Lotta Love," the rock anthem filled with raging fuzz tones, rumbling bass, thundering drums, and raw and sexual vocals. Dad sat there like a statue.

When the song ended, I turned down the volume, smiled at him and said, "Well?"

He looked at me and nodded. "It is a good song. I can see why you like it."

I could not tell if he was sincere or if he was playing the game. But I groaned. This was going to be impossible, it seemed.

However, Dad had an epiphany on a business trip a few months later.

"I had dinner with a colleague's friend," he said. "This man trained for twelve years as a doctor. Then he walked away from it."

"To do what?" I asked.

"To become.... a reporter."

"Really?"

"Yes. He said he never wanted to be a doctor, but he did it to make his family happy. But I do not want to see that happen to you. I do not want you to lose twelve years of your life. If you are going to be a reporter, go for it, and be the best reporter of all."

CULTURAL COLLISION 8: Let's not get *too* American

As for Mom, she had 2.6 children, along with a cozy house in glamorous California. However, she was bored. She'd had long afternoons over many years designing dream houses that we would live in someday. No such houses had materialized. She announced that she felt trapped and wanted to return to Islamabad, where she could at least tend to our income properties.

Dad was crestfallen. "I thought we were having a good ride. We've been pioneers. No Pakistani family has come so far," he said in a minor exaggeration. I would attempt to convince him that her comments were an indicator of mere boredom and not an indicator of oppression.

Ferhan also was feeling disconnected in California and was happy to go home with her. He was not part of the cool crowd and was oddly isolated at school, despite his winsome personality and Shabi's efforts to mold him into a model American child.

Mom was happy to take him with her, given how she and Dad suspected that Shabi and I were becoming too Americanized—and that Ferhan could profit from more time in the motherland.

The surprise was that I, who so often ran from Pakistan, now pondered going back too. I had learned to be comfortable enough in Islamabad, and I especially wanted to attend the American school there, which was small, cozy and less likely to cause an introvert like me to slip through the cracks. I could be a big fish, or at least a medium-sized one, in that tiny pond. Suddenly, all the consumerism that had me worshipping America seemed less important. I found myself willing to walk away from California.

Yet when Mom and Ferhan left, sometime in late 1981, I stayed, and Dad and I ended up having a good deal of time to talk. As I moved further into adolescence, we had more time to argue about life, religion and politics.

One Sunday morning, I walked into the family room to flip on the NFL when I noticed Dad sitting there. He had been there most of the night, brooding over an argument he and I had about whether Prophet Muhammad was right about everything. For some reason I had been talking up Jesus, maybe because I had been fascinated by stories about and references to Jesus' pacifism, especially after watching the movie *Gandhi*.

"I worry that we're losing you," he said. I seemed to myself to be in no danger of imminently becoming a Jesus freak. What was occurring was a drift into agnosticism. The whole idea of a noisy and meddling God seemed far-fetched, as did the notion that he only showed himself to a few privileged prophets and the notion that anyone outside my tradition was a heretic. Santa Claus, God, Buddha, it all seemed odd to me. Everyone fought over whose constitution or tradition or religion was right. People sure seemed to like to fight.

Our South-Asian/Mideastern heritage certainly ennobled the concept of the just warrior. This seemed natural and decent to my father: "Don't start a fight," he said. "But if the other person starts it, you must fight back hard."

People sure did love to fight. As a high-schooler, I watched toughguy talk from Ronald Reagan, who took office in the midst of an escalating Cold War. I brooded about the folly and futility of human conflict. I regretted how two sides could go to battle equally convinced of their moral superiority, and how one side's victory never brought a lasting peace. Human history was merely a long war with a few peaceful interludes, Churchill observed, and I'd have readily agreed as a 16-year-old.

At the Walden Books at the Thousand Oaks mall, I purchased hippie liberal Robert Scheer's "With Enough Shovels," which documented how Reaganesque hawks believed a nuclear war could be fought successfully by digging some holes and riding out the radiation. I believed that all signs pointed to human extinction. I supported a nuclear freeze. And I wondered if someone like me could get involved in protest movements.

At school, an unrepentant hippie professor, Mr. Hertz, helped some other students form a new club called the Nuclear Society. I signed up enthusiastically. The club quickly broke up when it turned out that the leaders weren't necessarily anti-nukes, and simply wanted to examine the issues without taking sides. Mr. Hertz and I had no time for that.

• • • • • • • •

I chose to attend the nearby University of Southern California, despite cautions from Mr. Hertz, who dismissed it as a rich white kids' school. But I knew it had a great journalism school, and I intended to be a great journalist, as Dad had charged me to do. I walked past the offices of the *Daily Trojan* and nodded confidently, "I'll someday be the editor of that paper."

I tried it on for size as a cub reporter for the Daily Trojan, and I found that I hated it. I sat in my dorm room and napped (I still appreciated that old pastime), stalling for time whenever the editors assigned me a story. One of my "highlights" as a reporter was a story headlined "Cracks in new sidewalk are normal, USC officials say."

My reporting classes further spooked me away from journalism because I had to do awful things such as asking rude questions and finding facts from people who did not want to talk. After much hand wringing, I changed my major emphasis from print journalism to broadcast management, which had nothing to do with reporting. And I later turned to public relations, which was similar to journalism but did not require rudeness or facts.

Shabi went on to move and shake within the mortgage industry, which left Ferhan as the family's final chance of producing even one measly doctor. He was up for the challenge—which was ironic, given that Dad no longer seemed to care. "Do whatever you want," Dad would tell him. Ferhan decided he wanted to make them happy by being a doctor. More on that later.

After I graduated from USC, they wanted me to at least earn a master's degree, though, and I was uncooperative here too. "It won't help me in the stuff I do," I insisted. "Are you crazy?" they countered. I had gotten a job at USC that offered me all sorts of chances to take free classes. Here my stubbornness impeded me. But it was a pattern that would affect other life choices in which my parents felt they had a stake.

Each summer during college, I traveled to Pakistan, spending time with Mom and Ferhan and often with Dad, who had begun to spend more time there. I was gratified by my trip to Islamabad after my freshman year. Having "found" my look and image for the first time in my life, I drew considerable adulation from my relatives as a dead ringer for Imran Khan, the former cricket-playing superstar (and now a politician) who had feathered hair that was almost as pretty as mine. This was the last summer in which my hair would withstand the pressure of male pattern baldness—in other words, my first and last moment of unadulterated glory.

On another trip 15 years later, my grandmother burst out laughing, "Oh, he's lost his hair!" Indeed, it is harder to hide an imperfect (*i.e.*, Pakistani) nose when you have got less hair to frame it appropriately. But looking American—looking Anglo—was something that we all craved.

II: Jesus Saves

CULTURAL COLLISION 9: Jack & Coke & Dad & Me

By the time I was a sophomore at USC, peer pressure would mingle with a diminishing fear of the Bully in the Sky and a skepticism that alcohol was as bad as Dad made it sound or as dumb as the high school partiers made it sound. I unbuckled myself from the constraints of my family and decided I could have a small shot of fun. While my roommates were at a movie one night, I pulled out one of their bottles of vodka and nervously poured myself a small glassful.

I took a sip, I gagged, and my head caved in. I rinsed my traumatized mouth out with water, milk, whatever was available. Never had a more malicious substance crossed my lips. It was unreal how bitter the vodka tasted. *This* was the much-vaunted alcohol that was the foundation of Western civilization and the key to getting laid? What were they thinking?

[Sophisticated drinkers will note, of course, that I was merely drinking the cheap, college-level vodka, not the costly stuff. Whereas the cheap spirits are spectacularly foul, the top-shelf ones are so minimally acrid by comparison that one would describe Grey Goose or Belvedere as "wonderfully smooth." It is a costly way to get drunk and to feel "grown-up" about it, but that is the system we have been given, and it will have to do.]

∙ ∙ ∙ ∙ ∙ ∙ ∙

Peer pressure being the force that guides the cosmos, what could have been my gag of alcohol was just the first of many. I managed to drink beer, but it was a passionless affair, because it tasted too much like earwax. I appreciated Long Island iced teas because they did not taste like death on the rocks and they swiftly gave me a sense of well-being.

During my time as a senior-year college intern on Capitol Hill, I missed the last subway train home, and blurred by the Long Islands, I unwisely decided to walk home. I strutted and stumbled past street gangs at 2 a.m., sat on darkened street curbs to catch my breath, walked a few miles too far and had to loiter on hotel couches to catch my breath again, and arrived at home at 4:30 a.m. with mysterious bruises on my legs. If Dad could see me now.

The contest: no, not the Seinfeldian kind

A few months later, he did get to see me in such a state.

I'd realized by now that I had an unusual capacity to down Jack Daniels straight, which provided me with a good portion of the peer acceptance I'd always craved. Any sissy could drink beer. But Jack straight? That made me a one-man party machine.

I had been waging a drink-off one night with my friend Dave, and had been getting the best of him—me swigging a bottle of Jack Daniels and him swigging his Tequila. We made sparklingly inebriated conversation, and he conceded victory at 11:30 p.m., at which point I had finished two thirds of my bottle and he had managed to suck down less than half of his. As a victory jig, I downed the rest of my bottle, which is the last moment I can clearly remember from that side of midnight.

The next thing I remembered was waking up in the George Washington University Medical Center emergency room, with a wall clock reading 2:30 a.m. My first reaction was, "Holy crap—I must have lost the contest." I ripped away a few tubes that were connected to my chest, and fled in an attempt to outrun any medical bills. Reeking of vomit, I hailed a taxi home. The poor cabbie could be forgiven if he killed himself later for sinking so low as to haul a puke-crusted bum like me around town.

Dave was still at my apartment, and his girlfriend Amy had joined him. They explained that Dave had called paramedics because, soon after finishing the bottle, I began losing consciousness and vomiting.

I listened to them while I changed into some shorts, and all the while my head throbbed without mercy. I jumped into bed and they wished me good night. Dave then mentioned, "Hey, will your Dad be freaked out about his conversation with you tonight?"

"What the…? What conversation? What are you talking about???" My heart jumped into my throat and lay there.

"Just after you downed the last part of the bottle, the phone rang and you answered it…"

"Ohmigosh, what the hell was I thinking? Why would I answer the phone then???"

"…And it was your Dad. And you looked like you were starting to lose it, and you were just mumbling. And you then just hung up and started puking."

Why would Dad call at such a late hour anyway? Had he suspected some Americanesque shenanigans?

With Dave's poignant narration, the scene was starting to come back to me. I could dimly recall an alarmed Dad asking, "What's wrong? What is going on?" And all I could do was sputter, garble and mutter. And I could recall hanging up in drunken resignation. "Oh, crap, oh, crap," I kept saying as the details came back into focus. "That's it. My life is over." Even still, it was not hard to fall asleep after my exhausting night.

• • • • • • •

The phone rang early the next morning, and I was somehow able to answer it, despite a bleary and lead-headed feeling. Surprise—Dad was again on the line. I snapped to attention as he informed me he would be coming right over from a friend's house at which he was staying in nearby northern Virginia. Dave and Amy scrambled to help me hide the alcohol bottles under the sink and clean up a bit, then wished me luck as they left.

I waited outside the building for Dad. He parked, then walked up to the building with stern determination.

"Hey, let's go to McDonald's," I said as cheerfully as I could. "Gawd,

I'm really hungry." I was not, but I needed to lie. I could not let him go to my apartment.

No dice. "Let's go to your apartment," he said with gravity.

Fortunately, the fragrance of alcohol had been masked well by the smell of vomit. But he snooped around the apartment anyway. Then, under the sink, he found a grocery bag with the bottles of Jack Daniels and tequila (come to think of it, why didn't Dave and Amy take those with them?).

My life would have flashed before my eyes, but my head still hurt too badly and was not in the mood for anything to flash in its vicinity.

Dad sat on my sofa-bed. He was stone quiet.

How would he react? Would he hit me? Would he scream?

He burst into tears.

"Why?" he asked. "Were you trying to kill yourself?"

"Huh? No, Dad. No. Of course not."

He soon gathered himself and grew calm. We disposed of the bottles. We went to McDonald's, where I somehow managed to scarf down an Egg McMuffin, some coffee and some orange juice. And he asked me how I was. Somehow, after one of the greatest shocks of his life, he found it in himself to be a loving father, first and foremost. Judgment could wait. He wanted to know that I would be okay.

And I felt reasonably okay, even though some bizarre plastic button remained mysteriously attached to my chest. Even though I did not have the nerve to take the button off my chest for two weeks because I worried that my lungs might go flooding out some hole that it covered. I later received a $500 bill for the ambulance ride to the hospital and other services. I called Dad to tell him about it; after a pause, he said he would pay it.

In the clutch, Dad's heart always found it hard not to flow with compassion.

• • • • • • •

I brooded over whether I was in trouble or just needed to dial down the drinking a tad. Sure, my Muslim family saw all drinking as devil-inspired, but various friends and colleagues and even a personal physician at USC insisted that my drinking was normal for college.

At the same time, a politically correct social-work establishment within the university cautioned even the slightest immoderation during the college years was conclusive proof of addiction. Next thing I knew I was urged to go to AA meetings, which I did dutifully but with a sense of puzzlement.

I admire Twelve Steps—it's been at the vanguard of efforts to solve the mystery of life, by achieving a balance between controlling what you can control and letting go of what you can't control. They have an evangelical way about them, though—convinced that anyone who arrives on their doorstep is a lifelong recovering drunk who will suffer hell on earth if he ever escapes their communal bear-hug or tastes another sip of alcohol.

Religiously, I remained in an agnostic phase, while somewhat fascinated by new age enchantment like crystals and creative visualization. I resisted the idea of a religious renaissance in my life.

Yet the Twelve Steps program and its practitioners talked endlessly about the need to "surrender to a Higher Power"—to give over one's obsessive attempts to manipulate all aspects of one's world, to give up the exhausting delusion that one can make oneself and everyone else happy. At first, I thought they were exaggerating the link between manipulative tendencies and addiction or compulsion.

I found myself wandering the USC campus one day during my last semester, pondering an imaginary God who was somehow becoming more real. "God, I don't know if you're up there," I thought. "But if you are, I do need your help." After a lull of several years, I was willing to believe in some sort of higher power again. But I didn't exactly go running back to Islam.

Spiritual, not religious... yet

I wanted acceptance. I wanted to conquer my roiling anxieties and towering fears. I would overturn every rock in search of a solution. Even back at the age of 16, I talked Mom into giving me money to go to a hypnotherapist, who tried to rid me of my phobia of people.

I had scoured psychology books as I moved into young adulthood, and they helped somewhat. I read new-age books about beta states of consciousness and alternate realities. I attended new-age workshops on meditation and on neuro-linguistic reprogramming of the mind.

Late in college, I had carried crystal rock specimens in my car, purchased from the popular Bodhi Tree Bookstore on L.A.'s quirky Melrose Avenue. The gold-hued ones gave me confidence, reportedly. The purple ones made my thoughts deeper, the pink ones made my heart warmer, the clear ones effected world peace and healed my acne, I suppose. But I eventually found all of them to be a tad unreliable, pretty as they were.

Soon after graduation, I would become a fan of new-age guru Marianne Williamson, and I would go to hear her speak weekly in the late 1980s before she came to national fame. I noticed that there were hundreds of gay men who poured in to Unitarian churches and rented auditoriums to hear her speak—not a surprise, since they were wrestling with the ravages of the new AIDS phenomenon and Williamson was willing to minister to them in a way that the Church failed to. I also noticed that she was a smart-aleck, sharp-tongued observer of life, and relentless in her desire to practice unconditional love as she believed Jesus modeled it.

One Sunday evening in a Santa Monica Unitarian church, one of her patented witty sermons was interrupted by a neighbor who was enraged that members of her flock had partially blocked his driveway. He cursed and screamed and left a whole sanctuary scandalized. He then skulked off.

I waited for her to make a snarky comment that would take the tension out of the room. Instead, she softly looked out at us and enjoined everyone there to be mindful of the neighbors there. She quietly and graciously took the bullet, then moved on.

I was struck by how naturally this came to her, and I can only poorly describe her grace there. Her ability to make Jesus a compelling model for living made me curious to hear more about what the orthodox Christian tradition had to say about him, given that it seemed to be the historic steward of his teachings. So it was inevitable that I would find my way into a classic Christian church.

The move into church soon happened, through two friends whom I had first met at the USC journalism school—my former advisers, Denton Holland and Debra Ono.

Denton had unfashionably shaggy brown hair and glasses that made him look like a heavier but nicer David Letterman. He was a homespun, Midwestern fellow who was as authentically caring as anyone I would ever meet.

Debra was a pretty and stylish Japanese-American woman in her late twenties, an Asian Mary Poppins; she walked into the room and birds landed on her shoulder and tweeted, and not in the new media sense. She cared genuinely for all who came in her path. And when someone so special believed you were special, there were no two ways about it—you felt special.

In November of 1988, Debra's church, Evergreen Baptist, would inaugurate its new sanctuary. I accepted Debra's offer to attend with her and her husband. Even though these rotten Christians were quick to condemn nonbelievers to hell, they were even quicker to drag you into their church and away from said hell.

I soon ended up becoming a part of their social circle, and found myself attracted to the way in which their pastor, Ken Fong, could proclaim a God of unconditional and unmerited grace. As Ken discussed 1 Corinthians 13 and the famous call to love others unconditionally, I imagined, "These people must be free of so many problems, if they get to listen to this kind of stuff every week." (As it turned out, they discussed such stuff less often than the new-age heretic Marianne Williamson did, given their preference for squabbling about how everyone else is headed for hell in a heresy bucket).

Finding Jesus, and being outed for the trouble

Debra, like most evangelicals, was eager to help me find my way. She arranged for Pastor Ken to sit with me and speak in detail about theological matters. Ken was a wonderful guy, speaking eloquently and thoughtfully of forgiveness and reconciliation as the highest work of God—forgiveness between God and humanity, forgiveness and unconditional love among human beings. Such a God seemed to be the authentic source behind Jesus' shocking call to turn our cheek toward those who despise us. It resonated with me, especially with my Gandhi-esque, peacenik instincts.

I had many more questions in my head—about seeming contradictions in the Bible, about the implausibility of one religion being "the one true path," and so on—but my heart was open. Ken's co-pastor, Cory, wrapped up a sermon one October morning in 1989, and asked us to join him in a prayer expressing a trust and a faith in Jesus and a desire to start a new life. I added my silent assent to the silent prayer of the group.

The pastor then asked, "With your eyes still closed, if you have made a confession of your faith for the first time, could you just raise your hand so I can see you? Just raise your hand briefly."

I felt he was invading my privacy, but I figured, "Oh, what the hell," and raised mine.

"Good, good, I see a few hands," he said. "That's wonderful. Praise God, praise God. Would those of you who raised your hands come on up and let us pray for you?"

Christ almighty, I'd been outed, and I had only been a "believer" for twelve or thirteen seconds. I thought it was a weaselly "force their hand" move on Cory's part, but I felt just as weaselly about refusing to go up there.

This one hard-sell, "come out of the Jesus closet" moment would change my life forever—and I have gone back and forth about whether it was a crafty or conniving move on the part of Cory.

I felt I now had to walk to the altar in front of the congregation, whose eyes were now opened. Ken was delighted, and he took me aside after the service to pray for me. I sought to take all the claims of salvation at face value, pondering what it meant to have Jesus "prepare you a room in Heaven." I felt a certain warm feeling of peace, imagining as best I could what it's supposed to feel like when God allows you to "pass from death to life," in the words of the New Testament.

At home later, I began to wonder how I would explain all this to my family. Would I call them immediately, or would I wait a few months until I visited them in Pakistan?

I took long walks along Hermosa Beach, brooding over how events might turn out. I assumed I would be thrown out of the family. That horrified me, but it also seemed a necessary price to pay to be able to follow your own conscience.

Happy Mother's Day

Don't imagine that I came to bring peace to the world. I didn't bring peace, but a sword. I've come to turn "a son against father, a daughter against mother, a daughter-in-law against mother-in-law. A man's enemies will be those in his own home." Those who love their fathers or mothers more than me aren't worthy of me.

—Matthew 10

Anyone who has left behind homes and brothers or sisters or father or mother or children or property for me will receive a hundred times as much in this lifetime, and eternal life afterward.

—Matthew 19

Pastor Ken dunked me in the big baptismal pool at Evergreen Baptist Church some time after my formal public conversion.

As I went down into the water, I found myself saying, "Bismilla hiraman niraheem." Or, "In the name of God, the Almighty, the Compassionate the Merciful." That was the invocation used by Muslims around the world. And it was an illustration of the peculiar road I would walk for years afterward, straddling a Muslim heritage and a desire to "follow the way of Jesus" or to be "a disciple of Christ."

It just happened to be Mother's Day, so all my church friends hugged me warmly, then went off to entertain their own mothers. I sat later in my apartment and pondered how Mom, then still in Pakistan, would feel about my treachery if she only knew.

Luckily in Pakistan no one even realized it was Mother's Day, since Hallmark is less active there.

CULTURAL COLLISION 10:
We don't care who the reason for the season is

A foolish boy brings sorrow to his father and anguish to the one who carried him.
—Proverbs 17:25

South Asia boasts a nice number of Muslims and Hindus who can't stand each other. But a few of them managed to break off and find Jesus, then strategize how to convert the others.

My pastor Ken soon introduced me to an Indian pastor and theologian, Sam Chetti, who understood and could navigate me through the complexity of my situation.

"Here's the main thing," Sam said: "You're not a Christian—you're a Muslim who puts his faith in Jesus."

"Umm…. Really? How does that work?" I understood that he wanted me to see myself in the same light that Jews for Jesus see themselves—faithful adherents of their old religion who find the fulfillment of their religion in Jesus.

Christian evangelicals see Jews for Jesus as a powerful model for how to combine the "salvation" of Jesus with one's own traditions. But I also knew that most traditional Jews don't trust Jews for Jesus as far as they can chuck them, and they wish they could chuck them further. In the end, no tribe likes losing members, even if the process is sugar-coated.

"But you won't be carrying the baggage of 2,000 years of white Christendom," Sam responded. "You don't need to be explaining away the problems of the Crusades, you just can speak truthfully about how you see the grace of God in Christ."

It was an intriguing point, but I rejected it nonetheless. I knew I hadn't been much of a Muslim, that I hadn't been a happy or productive trout swimming in the mainstream of Muslim culture. Why kid anyone? I found it easier to just come out and say I was now a Christian.

I gradually began telling friends and colleagues about my conversion. My roommate Jeff, who was happily atheist, thought I'd flipped. He had known me as a dabbler and spiritual dilettante, so he was puzzled and troubled that I would publicly convert to one faith—especially one that was seen as a rival to my family's faith.

I went to a movie in Westwood with Shabi and used the meeting as a chance to send up a trial balloon by casually floating the news that I was now a Christian. He paused, then muttered, "Geez, well, just don't tell mom and dad—it'd kill 'em."

The house lights dimmed, as did my mood. I brooded in the dark, and I can't even remember what film we saw that night.

I spent weeks torn between jealously guarding my prerogative to believe whatever the hell I wanted to believe and ruing how much my family would be hurt by the public aspect of my profession of a new faith—a faith that was seen as the chief proselytizing rival to their own vigorously proselytizing religion.

One Sunday afternoon I returned to the two-bedroom bachelor's pad that Jeff and I shared in Hermosa Beach, and decided I shouldn't wait until my upcoming trip to Pakistan that winter to announce my conversion.

I called Dad that Sunday for another one of our lousy phone conversations.

He had been on a business trip in Washington, D.C., and may have been staying at the same friend's house that he was at when he discovered I had befriended Jack Daniels.

Dad answered the phone and we exchanged pleasantries. He asked me how I had been.

"Good. Um. Oh, and today, I went to, uh, uh, church...."

"Hmm. What...?"

"I, uh, went with some friends today, to uh, church. Church."

"Oh.... Well." He paused and hesitated. "Oh. Well, just be careful when they talk about 'the son of God.' It is wrong to believe that God would have a son."

"Um. Well. Actually...."

"What? You don't believe it!"

"Um. Well, I think there's something to it."

"No!" He was devastated. "No! You cannot!"

"But I do."

"You do not! Say you do not!"

"I do, Dad, I'm sorry. I believe it."

I forget what he said next. However, he hung up on me a few seconds later. Then he called again, distraught. We repeated essentially the same conversation, but with more shock and emotion. He hung up again.

My roommate Jeff asked me how the conversation went.

"I think I just got kicked out of my family."

"Geez. Bummer. Well. Hey, let's go get some dinner."

"Okay." I was emotionally demolished, but I could still use the food and the company.

The next day, I was surprised to get another call.

"It is me," my dad said, composed and calm. "So. Are you coming to visit us in Pakistan during the holiday break?"

"Do you still want me to?"

"Of course."

"Then I'll be there. Thanks, Dad."

I would soon go to dinner at the home of Sam Chetti, the Indian pastor, and his family. His visiting father, a Christian preacher in India who gained respect for ministering to disease-infested families who'd been abandoned by local Hindus, would pray boldly that my entire family would be "saved." I thought this to be quite cool—we were taking the offensive in this religious battle.

I soon sent off a letter to my mother announcing my conversion while attempting to emphasize how much I still loved her and how she shouldn't feel like an incompetent mother.

· · · · · · ·

I had always envied how Christians had so much fun in America during Christmas—the warmth of the holiday cheer and the mystique were attractive. But now, my first Christmas as a Christian would be spent in Pakistan.

The time came to visit my parents, who were living in Islamabad. (Once Shabi and I had grown up, they tended to move back and forth between the two countries).

The two-week trip in December of 1989 was a serving of hell, served cold. British Airways was running late on the initial Los Angeles to London leg, and there was a strong chance that I would miss my connection in London.

I prayed to God that I would. But he did not smile on me then, and it was left for me to take up my cross and haul it across Heathrow Airport, as an airline staffer forced me and five other passengers to run a half-mile, with our baggage, to the Islamabad-bound flight. We made it in time, much to my annoyance, because I would dearly have loved to wait the five days necessary to catch the next flight. A chance to see London. A chance to explore. A chance to have five less days of unpleasantness with my family.

No such luck. I arrived in Pakistan, but my luggage did not. My parents and I somehow missed each other at the airport (in the age before cell phones), and I ended up catching a cab to their home. The air was not merely colder than in Islamabad's sweltering summers; as a Christian now, I felt that the very oxygen was thick with Islam, dripping with Islam, saturated in its culture and its ways.

Calls to prayer from nearby mosques rang out hauntingly at all times. The art, calligraphed writing and thinking of Pakistan are all heavily influenced by Muslim Arab life. Practically every sentence that Pakistanis utter ends in "Inshalla," meaning, "If God wills it."

My parents' house was a five-bedroom, three-story, cumin-scented building made out of concrete and covered with marble. As hot as Pakistan is during the summer, the heavy stone construction makes such structures cold as the lowest ring of Dante's Inferno during the winter; turn off your bedroom's gas heater for even a moment and your room is chilly again.

When my peeved parents arrived home after we unwittingly missed one another at the airport, they were several degrees cooler than the winter air, and just as Islamic. I tried to be warm and chummy, giving them a pair of high-quality pens and saying, "Merry Christmas, Mom and Dad."

Mom coolly put the pens away. "Christmas," she mumbled. "Christmas…. As if we want to celebrate Christmas."

I groaned—that was quite thoughtless of me. Christmas wasn't anathema to Muslims, but in this context any reminder of Jesus pricked at raw nerves. The fact that they were "Cross" pens may not have been appropriate symbolism either.

Mom was coughing up her lungs all day long, and had been sick for two months—roughly from the time she received the letter from me copping to my conversion. She seemed like she was going to die at times. It is always hard to lose a parent, but to be directly responsible is another predicament altogether. Dad would look at her hacking away, glance at me, and then shake his head.

Point, counterpointed—over and over

On a dreary and gray afternoon on the second day of the trip, we talked awkwardly in his bedroom. "Someday," he observed with cool gravity, "you will have a child. And you will look that child in the eye. And that child will look back at you." Now he spoke more slowly and softly. "And you will realize that, someday, that child will ruin your life the way you ruined mine."

Even having braced myself for hard conversations, I was not ready for that sort of conversation. I grew glum and somehow managed to continue the conversation. I do not remember anything else about that day. And truthfully, I was not as crushed by that as one might expect, because I knew Dad was all about cheap drama and themes of betrayal and gloomy romanticism.

He and Mom came at me in waves, over and over. Why, why, why, they demanded to know.

"Why did you have to reject your heritage?" Mom asked tearfully.

"Why do you hate us so much?" Dad asked.

"I didn't set out to reject anything, Mom and Dad."

Was I being fully honest?

I continued. "My believing in Christ gives me a real, um, peace."

"Peace?!?!?" Dad howled. "Peace?! So you want peace. But we will never again have peace, thanks to you. But you have your peace. Very good."

Put in those terms, peace did seem like a mere vanity.

Dad continued. "Why should a person ruin his family by accepting another religion? Everyone should respect and maintain the religion he was born into."

"How?" I shot back. "If that were the case, no one would ever have converted to Islam. Someone had to be the first in every family tree."

"That's different," Dad said. I rolled my eyes.

Second-worst man alive, with a bullet

At breakfast one morning, Dad was putting a little butter on his toast, while I was marmalading my own toast, and he wistfully looked off into the distance and said with little emotion, "You are the second-worst man alive."

For some reason, I smiled. I thought, Oh, geez, this is going to be good. I paused, then asked: "So who's the first?"

"Salman Rushdie."

Salman Rushdie. The bad apple of Ayatollah Khomeini's eye, the object of Khomeini's fatwa death sentence, all because of a snide literary depiction of the Prophet Mohammed's wives. Salman Rushdie. I was in the great devil's company.

As a public relations person, I was aware of many ways to spin the situation. For instance, a Presbyterian might have seen my conversion and said, "God stirred up your heart, quickened your conscience, convicted you of your sins, and led you to ask him for divine grace and an eternal and full measure of life, despite family pressure."

Mom had her own spin: "You took the easy way. You rejected your culture, and you took an easy religion that gives you forgiveness whether or not you do anything."

Dad had his spin to counter mine. "You became a Christian because you wanted to please your friends Denton and Debra."

"That's not true, Dad! Most of my friends are atheists. I could have pleased a lot more people if I abandoned God totally."

But Dad's words would go on to keep me up at night. The allegations about Denton and Debra had merit. I was someone who longed to be accepted, to be normal, or "Normal," in the eyes of people I valued. (Did I trade in my family's acceptance for that of a segment of American society? I would mull that for many months, at 2 a.m. and 4 a.m. and at various moments during the day).

You're brainwashed, I'm just well-informed

"It is all my fault," Dad lamented. "I did not educate you enough about Islam."

"No, that's not true, Dad. I knew a pretty fair amount about Islam, but I just decided it wasn't what I wanted for myself."

"No, you're wrong. If you really understood Islam, you wouldn't have gone and done this."

"How can you say that? How can you say that you know it all? There are billions of people on this planet who are not Muslim. Are they all just stupid?

"They're different. They did not grow up knowing the truth. You grew up knowing it and you walked away. The punishment is heavier for you."

That made me shiver. He continued. "Robbie, I have heard of many, many Christians becoming Muslims, but I have never, ever heard of a single Muslim becoming a Christian."

"Dad, I've heard of lots of Muslims becoming Christians."

"No. Never."

Sigh. Neither of us had statistics we could cite, and it would not have mattered if we did.

My parents and I huddled near gas heaters in cold rooms and debated theology endlessly and pointlessly. I felt satisfied that I held my ground, but was irritated that I scored no points with them.

Still, I'd gone from the milquetoasty middle brother to the rebellious, stubborn black sheep of the family. That was kind of cool.

Meet the Mullah

Toward the end of this eleven-day Inquisition, Mom took me to the home of a religious scholar, where he pressed me about the inconsistencies of my faith, mostly by telling me I was a "dualist." I responded, "So what's wrong with that?" although I wasn't sure what a dualist was. He told me that I needed to reconvert back to Islam, or my family would be obligated to cut me off. I told him I did not plan to. He told me that ruling it out would be "intellectual suicide." There may have been truth in that, but I doubt he woke up each morning willing to consider converting to Christianity, Buddhism, Hinduism or any other ism.

(Years later I read about how Charles Templeton, an evangelist colleague of Billy Graham, told him during their early ministry days that Graham was committing "intellectual suicide" by refusing to go with Templeton to Princeton Seminary to do some objective study of Christian doctrine).

The remainder of my days there involved more dosages of guilt and sadness, as I watched my mother hacking away as though she might have only days to live. I also had a few talks with Ferhan, who had grown into a thoughtful and devout teen Muslim; he was alarmed by events and sought to engage me in long philosophical discussions. As I already felt worn down by my parents, I resisted extended debate.

As my trip grinded to an end, my parents seemed to declare a tense truce.

"We are not going to throw you out of the family," Dad said. "You'll always be a part of this family, for better or worse."

I appreciated this, yet had mixed feelings. I might have preferred to be tossed out at last. Let them get mad, let them publicly denounce me, let them cut me off, let them grieve, let them forget me and get a cat or a dog to replace me. And let me live my life.

Instead, they intended to remain a part of my life, which I realized would amount to their clinging to my leg and begging me to be less-than-public in my faith. How is that for a mixed blessing?

After all that, I was relieved to get on the British Airways 747 after 11 days of trial by blowtorch.

Let my rivals tremble

Some months later, my roommate Jeff—an atheist who kept my spirits up with his wry observations about the silliness of all this religiosity—burst into our apartment, holding up the front section of the *Los Angeles Times* and chanting, "We're number one! We're number one!" Puzzled, I took the newspaper from him, examined it, and found what he was referring to. "Rushdie Converts Back to Islam," read the headline.

I had apparently backed into the top spot, as the single worst man alive.

Jeff found the affair to be mostly amusing. Having known me since my angry high school days, and having seen my angry Marxist and indifferent atheist and spacey new-age and Taoist periods, he told me this was just another phase of my personal moon. That annoyed me.

"This is different," I said. "It's not a phase. It's kind of like what I was always searching for."

"Uh-huh."

"This is something happens to you when you're a Christian. I've got something now that's not just like a temporary thing."

"Sure"

At a deeper level, I was fearful that he was objective and that he would turn out to be right. Jeff was no dummy.

That newfound inner peace that I had boasted about to Dad while in Islamabad was an unreliable companion in the ensuing months. I had accepted a son of God who people told me was the embodiment of divine grace, but who had represented a supreme blasphemy during my childhood.

In my public relations job at USC, I was working with a producer from the KFWB-AM news radio station, who told me she moonlighted at a small Christian station in Orange County. I think the host of the show she produced was named something like John Stewart; I'd heard him deliver what seemed to be very authoritative commentaries on Biblical orthodoxy. She mentioned that he recently interviewed Marianne Williamson and had "really held her feet to the fire!!" I said I'd be fascinated to hear an interview in which such a traditionalist would cut up a heretic like Williamson. She sent me the tape, I popped it in expectantly, and found myself troubled and puzzled by what I heard. Far from having her feet held to the fire, she gently tried to make her points about the overriding importance of unconditional love while her host ridiculed her for not taking a high enough view of Biblical authority.

I thought back to seeing Williamson put unconditional love into true practice. And I felt that what she stood for would matter more to Jesus than what the radio host stood for.

Every sin is bigger in Texas

Mom and Dad were back in the States by the summer of 1990. They had sold our old house in northern Virginia and were looking for a business they could stick the equity into before the taxman got to it. Traveling the land, they found a suitable prospect: a run-down, foreclosed motel in Austin, Texas.

I had been summoned to visit them and to bring out our family's old, red Nissan Sentra, a crappy thing that lacked air conditioning and that had lost its fifth gear due to Shabi's maniacal tendencies behind the wheel.

The drive from L.A. to Texas is a miserable, dry and dusty one, unless you're one of those crazy people who gushes about how dry deserts are beautiful. Me, I mostly did nocturnal driving due to the lack of A.C. A few hundred miles short of Austin I settled in at 4 a.m. at a rest stop for a quick nap. During my sleep, I began to slip into a dream.

Standing before me was Jesus, looking bright, radiant and serene. I moved toward him with a sense of awe. I looked down, then looked up at him again. But he had turned into my mother.

I hate dreams.

Further, Mom, a.k.a. Jesus, was pointing to a sign next to her that said, "There is only one God, Allah, and Muhammad is his prophet." I gulped.

Next, I felt a powerful, dark presence hovering above me, as though it were ready to descend upon me and take me off to hell.

I woke up right there in that warm, early morning Texan desert—and started driving again.

Approaching Austin, the ride went from barren to lush. Rolling hills that reminded me of England greeted the rising sun, and a stop at a folksy general store made me feel as though I had stepped into a Disneyland Main Street attraction.

The moment of truth came, when I rolled up to the Austin motel—which was not nearly as crummy as I had feared. And I trundled up the stairs and knocked on the door of my parents' room, bracing myself for another trip marked by tensions, emotion and criticisms.

Dad opened the door; he smiled broadly and his eyes brightened. He gave me a crushingly loving bear hug, the kind that squeezed new life into you, as though the prodigal son had returned, and Mom was tearfully happy too. Beyond the trauma and the differences, they just missed their son. And they were thrilled to spend some time with me.

Religion did not come up, just the minutiae of life. I did make a faux pas though one night at the Black-Eyed Pea restaurant. Eating there with Mom, I foolishly ordered the red beans and rice, hoping she would not notice one of the ingredients in it. She looked up at me and quietly said, "So…. You eat pork." I said nothing. I had been an insensitive dork. I just didn't think she'd paid attention to the ingredients, which were listed on the menu.

As I got ready to leave Austin, Dad gave me an unexpected gift: a massive philosophy textbook. It was an interesting book, I will admit. But I suspected that Dad was hoping that, since a little independent thinking made me question Islam, a little more independent thinking might make me question Christianity. Sort of like in television sitcoms, when one bonk on the head gives you amnesia and the second bonk restores you to your senses.

Going Hollywood, evangelical-style

After a few years at Evergreen, Debra's church, which was mostly Asian-American, I felt drawn to Hollywood Presbyterian Church, of which my Indian mentor, Pastor Sam Chetti, had spoken highly.

Mom and Ferhan came to church with me on a couple of occasions. She told me that she liked Hollywood Presbyterian more than Evergreen, since it had the classic Gothic feel that contemporary Evergreen lacked. I suppose her thinking was that, if you're going to a church, go to one that at least looks like a sacred place. Evergreen looked like an oversized living room, lacking only the La-Z-Boy recliners.

During a visit to Hollywood that she and Ferhan made while he was in medical school, Lloyd Ogilvie was preaching a magnificent sermon on "losing oneself for the sake of Christ," and I noticed Mom sniffling and crying a bit. I do not think she was moved as much as she was just plain saddened that she was visiting a Christian church that her son called home. Ferhan was more stoic.

I managed to bring Ferhan during another visit of his, this time dragging him to a talk on the Sermon on the Mount by Tod Bolsinger, a gifted teacher-theologian prodigy who was one of my most important mentors. Tod spoke well about how Christ's sermon was intended to redirect one's attention from external deeds to the state of the heart, and that Christ was calling people to an intimacy with God more than to a list of duties. I thought Tod's talk was a wonderful response to many people's approach to Islam, which so often could seem to be focused on "do this and do that" legalistic regulations.

But Ferhan did not exactly cower and admit the superiority of a Christian approach to faith. "I agreed with basically everything your friend Tod said," he offered later at dinner. "We should focus on the state of our heart, not on our actions. But I just disagree with the idea that Jesus is God, or even the son of God. I don't see why I need to believe that or would want to believe that."

Within our family, I thought the war was handled with a certain civility and decency.

Indeed, despite the initial riot sparked by my conversion, the family managed to stay close. Mom went back to nagging me as much about how I should go to graduate school as about anything else. Dad asked me when I would hurry up and get married before I go completely bald, which sounded to me suspiciously like entrapment of a poor female sucker. Both he and Mom now accepted that marriage would not be to a Pakistani gal, due to the religious chasm, and they gave up trying to fix me up; now they just wanted me to hurry up and marry a pretty gal that would make for cute kids.

• • • • • • • •

One one visit to California in the early '90s, when she spent a few months as a houseguest at Shabi's place, Mom was in a contentious mood one night as she prepared dinner in his kitchen. She seemed angered by my distance from my heritage. She fretted about my singleness. And she seemed irritated by the idea that I had always scoffed at the sort of arranged marriage that was a foundation of her tradition.

I began to put two and two together. I looked at her and said, "This whole anger about me being another religion isn't really about some theological issue, is it, Mom? You don't really care about what I think about the Trinity. You're just mad that, the way things worked out, you won't be able to marry me off to some Pakistani girl."

Mom broke into tears. "Yes, that's right. You did just what you had to do to make that impossible."

I had no response.

Finding a place in the sun

"Care about people's approval, and you will be their prisoner," Steven Mitchell's translation of the Tao te Ching says.

"Everybody wants me to be what they want me to be, I'm not happy when I try to fake it," said the Commodores in that great song, "Easy."

As children, my brothers had spent countless evenings sitting near the feet of our parents as they lay in bed and talked about the future. We intimately knew their ambitions, which we should have worn like a suit. Dress like gentlemen, get straight As, get a full scholarship to Harvard, graduate at the top of our medical school class, bring great honor to our lineage, and then extend that lineage. We would live on the same street, and so on.

Like me, Shabi had no interest in becoming a doctor. He did reach the top of the mortgage profession, as a president of a mortgage company by his 40th birthday. He was a popular manager, beloved by his employees. He showed up one day at Mom and Dad's place with a small gift—a compact Mercedes C230. Mom and Dad were thrilled and proud.

My career was more of a puzzle to them. I had become the speechwriter for the president of USC. Not a bad gig, and it was a prestigious calling in the eyes of my work colleagues and my friends. But Dad used to tell friends that "Robbie is a, uh, a *journalist* at USC." I think he just struggled to grasp what it was that I did.

But as one who had chosen a life against his wishes, I always felt compelled to act and feel as though his approval didn't matter to me.

Shabi ended up marrying one of his employees. Maria was half-Anglo, half-Korean, and Christian, albeit in a low-key manner.

My parents fell like twin anvils. She doted on them, bought them gifts and took them to lunch. They were relieved, then tickled and delighted, that Shabi would date someone who accepted them fully.

Love, Pakistani-style and modern-style

Ferhan was a good boy in every sense of the term—a good student, a good son, a good Muslim who learned his Quran well, and who even wanted to become a doctor. He was not the kind of son that Robbie or Shabi grew into.

But he tempted fate. This lad who had pledged to serve his motherland forever could have enrolled in the Pakistani higher educational system, which would have given him a medical degree in several year's less time and at considerably less expense, but he and our parents wanted him to be the best doctor possible; and this required the best education possible. And so, in a recapitulation of Dad's journey, he came to America in 1992 for his undergraduate and medical education.

He had been admitted to Duke University and loved the idea of going there. But the word Duke also represents some kind of secondary position among royalty, and it is not a university to which a responsible Pakistani sends a child. Dad and Mom instructed him to go to Johns Hopkins; finally one of their progeny would attend a university that makes parents proud rather than puzzled.

Ferhan sailed through Johns Hopkins' pre-med program in three years, because Mom told him to hurry up and get it over with because tuition does not grow on trees. He did not even study much, but cranked out a 3.8 GPA. Next stop for him was Baylor Medical School in Houston, a top-20 school that wasn't quite Ivy League, but he'd hurt his chances at getting into an Ivy League school by rushing through his schoolwork without getting into any extracurricular activities.

He had many Pakistani friends at Hopkins, but fewer in Houston. Such friends made it easier to be a Muslim in America, especially since Ferhan was conservative enough to keep *halal* food standards, the Muslim equivalent of kosher. That means that most meats had to be sacrificed to God, which rules out most of the menu at McDonald's or anywhere else. At Johns Hopkins, this implied a diet of mainly pizza, coke and cake from the cafeteria.

His purity and zeal made a *halal* person out of Mom, but Dad valued his meat wherever he could find it, and wasn't about to sweat the small stuff.

Bizarro Rob meets Bizarro Krypton

What America does to immigrants, its sanitized northern counterpart does as well. In an old episode of *The Simpsons,* an Asian child gushes during a patriotic essay contest about his once-penniless immigrant family's rapid ascent. "Where else but America—or possibly Canada—could such a thing be possible?" he asks.

Canada, you may recall, was the land praised by Altaf, the Bizarro version of me whom I had met some years earlier in Islamabad.

Altaf relished informing his Yankee schoolmates, at some threat to his physical safety, that Canada was a superior civilization to the United States. Yet as proud as he was of Canada, he and his family even more proudly walked away from it, descending from its grand peaks to live in the valley of their homeland. And they considered me a fool for refusing to do the same.

Something happened on the long road home, though: You could squeeze the Pakistani out of Canada, but you could not squeeze the Canada out of the Pakistani.

His sister Amera, who had been so enthusiastic in bullying me to make Pakistan my home, was herself not able to make a home of her homeland. Many people in other countries typically start out with good intentions to stay close to and faithful to their motherland, but finally decide that they need an education that is only available in the U.S. or Canada. She did so. So off went Amera, still feeling the effects of Americanization via Canada, to get a little schooling—and ended up marrying a Caribbean gentleman.

When their father found out, his Vesuvian head blasted through the ceiling.

South Asians typically carry a certain racism. In the 2003 movie *Bend It Like Beckham*, the lead character, a teenage Hindu girl tells friends that she is forbidden from marrying white men—and that Muslims and black men are especially off limits. Further, people of various religions in the Asian subcontinent value lighter skin. That made fair-skinned Mom a demi-goddess by Pakistani standards.

Pakistanis would often remark upon seeing a fair-complexioned child, "Oh, she looks like she could be American." They would often give fistfuls of bonus points for beauty to otherwise homely persons who had light skin or bluish eyes.

Yet if a person has striking features but dark skin, he or she can be docked many points. I had heard tsk-tsks, as in, "tsk-tsk, that girl would have been wonderful marriage material if she just had lighter skin." Black Americans like to see Middle Eastern and South Asian people as brethren, but they would be crestfallen to find that the average white man in Alabama has a more progressive view of race relations than the average South Asian.

Why such a premium on fair skin? I do not buy that it is caused entirely by the influence of American media. Myriad cultures do associate fair skin with wealth, as the rich fed on grapes on couches indoors while the peasants got a full dose of Apollo in the fields. So it may be a combination of that, the influence of American media and envy over Western dominance.

But back to Altaf's father: When we last heard from him, he was flipping his lid, which remained flipped, twisted and tormented. He banned Amera from the family, which forced the rest of the family to commune with her secretly.

His torment mercifully did not last much longer. What was left of his heart shattered or imploded. When I heard the big bully had left us to go nag his neighbors in Hades, I didn't weep, though I can look back today and dimly recognize the sadness of it all. His background was not all that different from that of Dad. However, he was ultimately killed by it all, while Dad seemed to withstand the more perplexing aspects of life in North America.

Years later, Altaf tracked me down. Finding me through the Internet and phone directories, he called up one day, pronounced his name in a very Americanized—okay, Canadianized—way, and told me he was living in Toronto. The grand and permanent return to Pakistan had been short-circuited. He was involved in an on-again, off-again romance while finding work as a lawyer, as a writer—it was a Western, individualized existence.

In Tod we trust

I was becoming more active at Hollywood Presbyterian Church, which at one time was America's largest Protestant church—with about 9,000 members in the 1950s, back when every American adult found it necessary or advantageous to claim membership in a church. By the time I got there, it was about a quarter that size.

I became involved with BRICK (Building Relationships in Christ's Kingdom), a giggly and nervous Sunday class of about 80 young professionals who were led by Tod Bolsinger. Bolsinger was an extraordinarily gifted young Bible scholar and speaker who filled me with jealousy because he was so accomplished, so knowledgeable, yet only a year older than I.

I idolized Tod, who would go on to mentor me during the five years we spent together at BRICK and Hollywood Pres. He championed me as a leader in the church and helped me become intensely active at Hollywood. There, close to the clubs and bars of Hollywood Boulevard, I would spend many long afternoons and evenings at committee meetings while my peers built careers or families.

I considered it a privilege to play the role I played, though. This, I was convinced, was the Kingdom of God in action. Even with its many imperfections, it was a "foretaste of heaven," to use Tod's favorite expression.

Many BRICK members were transplants from other parts of the country, here in search of a career as screenwriters or directors. Others were schoolteachers or psychologists. Most were lonely, and intensely needed a sense of community (or "fellowship," to use the church term).

I already was satisfied with my friendships from USC and from high school. I came looking not for a community but for a wife. So I made an appointment to see Tod and to suggest that the class break into small group discussions that would facilitate getting to know one another, and would especially facilitate my meeting a hot chick.

Tod argued that too many people felt intimidated by small groups and preferred to make connections informally after class, or at their occasional parties. Before I knew it though, he signed me up to be on the BRICK leadership group, which stunned other members of this tight-knit class who didn't yet know who Rob Asghar was.

That would change my life, as I would spend the next dozen years tightly associated with that group. I resisted at first, shunning most of the events while still waiting for Ms. Right to walk into class each Sunday. Over time, however, I warmed up to the group, and they became like family. I dated a few of them, which could become about as messy as, well, dating within your family. Because of the messy dynamics, and because I aspired to be a leader, I was overly cautious about whom I would date and how far or fast I would advance. I certainly could have dated women more casually, inside and outside the church; but given how evangelicalism made extramarital sex such a taboo, my peers and I felt compelled to find life partners fast.

After I was named president of BRICK, two years into my membership there, one of my predecessors came up to me. "I guess I can tell you now, Rob, but when you first came to BRICK, someone told me, 'Keep an eye on this Rob guy—sometimes these Muslims like to infiltrate Christian groups.'" I chuckled, then tried guessing which right-winger said that. There were several, and they were always the ones who told me that the Bible needed to be taken literally. Interestingly, the more literally you take the Bible, the more likely you are to vote Republican, as Bill Bishop noted in his book, *The Big Sort*.

Years later, Barack Obama, for all his articulate pronouncements about the power of his Christian faith, would be suspected of being a "closet muzzie" and pseudo-American among right-wing message boards. Big surprise.

When the Lord gets too lenient

Much of the joy in my Christian life came from relationships with many big-hearted and bright people, some like Tod who took their theology seriously and many who took it with a grain of salt. I took theology very seriously, always trying to find ways to reassure myself that Christianity was sufficiently unique and correct to justify my scandalizing my Muslim family.

The other high point in my Christian journey involved pivotal Christian images that inspired me through the muck of life. The notion of an incarnate God who took the suffering of the world upon himself, to the point of death, gave me a model that was quite helpful while dealing with idiots in my church or my workplace. The notion of an infinitely giving and forgiving God, modeled in Jesus, seemed remarkable—yet I was always puzzled and confounded by how many Christians didn't take the forgiveness-and-reconciliation angle seriously, either within church political battles or within American political battles. Many seemed to be far more worried about formulas for how to "save the lost" from hell, or about defending their theory of Biblical authority or about taking a stand on abortion or about various lists of moral codes that "faith in Christ" required. Conservatives often had strict codes about sex and occasionally alcohol, while liberals often had strict codes against materialism and in favor of "social justice." Conservatives saw the devil in Hollywood, and liberals saw the devil in Wall Street, but neither side seemed great at forgiveness and "enemy-loving" as Jesus seemed to prescribe in the Sermon on the Mount and as he seemed to model on the Cross.

If confronted, both sides usually had an alibi for why they didn't live up to Christ's standards in enemy-loving or turning the other cheek—they claimed that humans are fallen and will never live up to Christ's standard of perfection. The problem was that, in the clutch, many of my friends, as well as national church leaders, seemed far more worried about "correcting" themselves in other areas but not in this one. In other words, no one in the church genuinely believed that they were at fault. Even while taking the idea of human imperfection seriously, it sometimes made me wonder if the all-powerful God really had his ducks in a row, or if he was genuinely comfortable cheering on his followers when they turned opportunities for reconciliation into cosmic struggles in which they were good and their opponents were evil ones to be smited.

Sure, there were many forgiving exemplars inside the church. There were many outside the church too. Here again, Marianne Williamson seemed more intent on taking Christ's words seriously than most evangelicals, even though evangelicals would dismiss her as a heretic. The point was that some nights I wondered if theology really mattered—and if it didn't, why did I use that as a wedge between myself and my family?

Make disciples of all nations, except the one you're from

A Chinese-American friend, Sabrina, had longed to get a missions assignment in her homeland, and she was horrified that I had no intention of finding a similar assignment in Pakistan, using my familiarity with that culture to Jesus' strategic advantage.

But she knew little about my tense relationship with that culture, with my fondness for American consumerism, and my general discomfort with Pakistan.

"I think we're all called to different things," I responded, using that "call" word that I was normally suspicious of due to people's use of it to sanctify their dumbest decisions. "I'm not necessarily going to be a missionary just because I'm Pakistani. Some white Americans feel more called to live in Pakistan and to talk about Jesus there. I feel called to live in California and do writing and things over here."

Beyond not wanting to give up the creature comforts of California, I had theological concerns. In the spirit of Jesus ominously calling his followers to deny themselves and take up their crosses, I was quite willing to be shot, but only for my own principles, not for the principles or doctrines or dogma of others. And I was still wrestling with parts of what I was supposed to believe.

And I also wondered if I might find encouragement for an arduous life of missions through the appropriate kind of wife—a woman who'd not only be great in the sack, but who'd be a good "partner in ministry." Many prayer-warrior elders at Hollywood assured me that God had such a plan for me. I waited and prayed.

I tended to frown upon the many people in church who clung to the notion that God is a cosmic Santa Claus who can be worn down by whining. As much as the Bible seemed to offer promises about how God would bless us with wonderful things, I believed it was imprudent to expect too much. I felt this way partly because I had been so immersed in Eastern, "go with the flow" thought, which was as content to adapt to circumstances as to change circumstances. I found Biblical scriptures that indicated that the promises weren't to be taken at face value.

But I believed that the promises did indicate some real hope of divine intervention in our lives, and my personal hopes were limited to two areas: That God would bring a special woman into my life, and that Jesus would enter into the heart of my family, vindicating my own religious choices.

Yet being children of an arranged marriage put Shabi and me at a competitive disadvantage in the Darwinian world of courtship. "We don't have any role models for dating," Shabi once complained to Mom.

It went past dating knowledge; I did not know how to express any romantic feelings. So we both dated rarely, and more often than not ended up in Friendship Purgatory. I had my share of romantic "successes," but I spent far more time attempting to redeem the failures.

Ferhan didn't have to worry about this. In his third year of medical school at Baylor, he became engaged to get married. This was an arranged marriage, another recapitulation of Dad's own life. Mom had set this marriage up after scouring Islamabad for good prospects, which resulted in Ferhan and a 19-year-old named Pakeeza choosing each other.

This was Pakistani Love, Late 20th Century Style. Our family had been friends over the years with Pakeeza's family, and Pakeeza was almost like a daughter to Dad, who brought her small gifts and tokens whenever he visited Islamabad. So Ferhan and Pakeeza were not strangers in the way that Mom and Dad were on their own wedding night.

Time and technology had caused other refinements in the arranged marriage system. Ferhan, in the U.S., and Pakeeza, in Pakistan, were able to get to know one another better during their engagement through the magic of e-mail. And in the fall of 1998, the date of their wedding festival in Islamabad would finally arrive.

By then, I had become a small-time mover and shaker at Hollywood Presbyterian. I was elected an elder, thanks to the championing of my mentor Tod, and I was the chairman of the church's missions committee, thanks to my ill-fated pursuit of a missions-minded girl named Kate. As missions chairman, I was one of the church's main persons in charge of trying to bring salvation to the teeming masses. This made it awkward when I returned to Islamabad for the wedding in November of 1998, nine years after the hellish post-conversion visit there.

Jesus Freak returns to Islamabad

Upon my arrival in Islamabad, the air seemed as thick as ever with Islam. For what seemed like the umpteenth time, British Airways lost my luggage. But this time, my folks were much cheerier in their approach to me. Mom once again was sick, but this time she was just sick with anxiety about the wedding.

As a Pakistani wedding drags on for days, much of that time is spent standing still posing for pictures with the new couple. Even in the day of video cameras everyone stands still, which made little sense. Day after day, we stood still. But the food was usually excellent. Piping hot breads, aromatic stews, tandoori-grilled chicken to die for. It makes the whole marathon worthwhile.

My relatives were eager to see me, eager to tease me about losing my hair, and just downright flattered that "the American guy" seemed happy to be around them as they were with me.

Our five-bedroom house in Islamabad was jammed with about 30 visiting relatives; they were almost popping out of the windows of the overstuffed house. And they would stay up until 2 a.m. every night singing, playing bongo drums and dancing. It was exhilarating and exhausting.

Most importantly, I felt more at peace with my identity than in years past. I was a Pakistani-American, for better and for worse. Making peace with that allowed me to be less defensive about myself and to enjoy my relatives more thoroughly than ever before. They seemed to notice the difference, too.

A more evangelical believer than I was at that time would have used the opportunity to say, "You know, I'm the missions chairman at my church, and I feel a special calling to share with you the love and grace of Christ Jesus, so that you might have peace in your heart and the gift of eternal life. And if you're not willing to do that, how would you like to contribute to our missions fund, which badly needs your investment?"

I brought no such strategy. It would have destroyed the festivities and possibly would have resulted in the cancellation of the wedding by Pakeeza's family. I felt called to love them, not to preach to them. (Of course, I should add that that was my tendency even when dealing with unbelievers in the United States).

You look good in a closet

Though Pakeeza was sick as a dog when I met her at a dinner event at the Islamabad Club, she was gracious and attractive. Her four younger sisters were beautiful as well; it was a fetching family.

The nikka was performed on the first night of festivities, just before the mandhi. The mullah, an incredibly serious and dour holy man, asked for a vow from Pakeeza, who was on the female side of the room, then he prayed for her and blessed her and asked her to sign some forms. Next, he moved to the male side of the room, where he did the same with Ferhan. A group of men sat around and prayed during this time. Look closely at the wedding video and you might be able to see me glancing furtively at everyone else, to see when I was supposed to be raising my hands and so on.

Then the men embraced and congratulated Ferhan. Mom came over and hugged him. He was now a married man, although about two hundred other men and women had no idea what was going on, did not care, and were busy yammering while eating finger foods. It is as different from the climactic "I do" and "kiss the bride" moments as you could have at a wedding.

However, once the nuptial bureaucratic hurdles were cleared, the party began in earnest. Young women and girls from the bride's side and the groom's side performed a sort of dance-off, showing off their respective abilities during song numbers that had been choreographed and rehearsed in preceding weeks. The grim-faced mullah sat in the back, seeming to be wishing that his friends from the Taliban were here to slap some good old-fashioned sense into the crowd of reprobates.

Ferhan and I were driving home from an Islamabad restaurant a few days later. "So does Pakeeza know I'm a Christian?" I asked.

"Nope."

"Oh. You haven't told her?"

"Uh-uh."

"Oh. When are you going to tell her?"

"Actually.... I wasn't planning on telling her."

"What? Really?"

"Yeah. It would freak her and her family out. It's your private life. Just no need to get into it."

"Huh? Hmnm... Well." I was annoyed. Was I now going to have to conceal what seemed to be a pivotal part of my life, the part of it that I was constantly talking about and living out? That was not going to be easy.

Pakeeza and I did get to talk a little in my parents' home, a day or two before I returned to the States. "So are you interested in getting married someday?" she asked me.

"Um, yeah. We'll see, though."

"To an American? A Pakistani?"

"Um. Dunno."

"Can I ask if religion's a factor for you in who you'd marry?"

"Yeah…. It is…. But not in the way that it is for Ferhan."

"Oh. Uh-huh."

I thought that would give her a hint, and I believed I gave her other hints in the subsequent months after she joined Ferhan in the U.S. But she suspected nothing. No one leaves Islam. Certainly not for Christianity. So there was nothing for her to suspect, as far as she was concerned.

A year later, she was living in Houston with Ferhan, as he was finishing his education at Baylor Medical School. My parents lived with them too. I went out to visit all of them once, and as she and I drove around town one day, she pointed out, "That Shell station that you see is operated by a Muslim. I go to him, figuring that I'd rather give our money to him than to some Christian." I grumbled under my breath, but I kept my mouth clamped up tight.

Faith is only confusing when you think about it

At the same time, I occasionally sat at sermons and Bible lessons and found myself struggling to cram mental square pegs into mental round holes. Did Jesus consistently believe he was the son of God? Why did the Old Testament seem so oblique in its prophecies about the Messiah? Had God's character changed between the time in which he commanded Israelites to kill every last Caananite and the time in which Jesus spoke of saving every last sheep of his kingdom? Sometimes I thought to myself, "I have to get up and leave here." Sometimes that happened even while I was teaching a Bible lesson.

A true ham, even if a shy ham, I loved to teach lessons at church. Some people noticed that I used a lot of wisdom from outside the Bible, as opposed to just teaching the Bible. That was an astute observation of how, while I had a strong command of evangelical theology, I always struggled with the many contradictions of the Bible. Given how deeply others loved the Bible, I suspect that reduced the demand for me as a teacher. I could not bring myself to sell them what they most wanted to purchase.

One friend, a woman deeply committed to the community of Hollywood Pres but a quiet skeptic like me about many issues, noticed one Sunday morning that I had a copy of Lao Tzu's Taist classic, the Tao te Ching. She chuckled. I smiled. It was a heresy of sorts, especially for a church elder such as myself. But whenever I was distressed or confused, I went to the Tao te Ching for solace. Rarely the Bible. If I ran to the Bible, I was overwhelmed with its contradictions and implausible stories. Therefore, I could only run to it when I was in a good mood. The Tao, by contrast, was a source of serene meaning, offering a sense of grandeur amidst its poetic view of the cycles of life and death and high and low and yin and yang. Reading the Tao te Ching, I could see death as a natural successor to life, without feeling compelled to ponder how bacteria, parasites and other death agents would have been introduced into the universe after the fall of Adam. But few Christians knew that about me.

They like me, they really like me

Ferhan and Pakeeza soon moved off to the University of Michigan in Ann Arbor for an orthopedic residency after he wrapped up his medical studies in Houston. Mom and Dad treasured the Pakistani notion of parents and progeny living in one household, but not if five months of snow was involved annually.

They pondered the next-best option. On a visit to my older brother's home in Orange County, my folks began discussing a permanent return to California. Shabi was in favor of the idea and had been urging them on.

"What would you think of that, Robbie?" Dad asked.

"Well, you know I'm pretty busy," I said. "I can't necessarily drop everything and come visit you twice a week."

"That's okay," my mother said. "Just visit when you can."

"Well… Okay," I said. "But you know I also live my life in a way that you don't necessarily approve of."

"Well," Dad said. "We have seen how you live, and we believe it is the way of Islam."

I was caught off guard. "Islam" means submission to God. Dad thought that, despite our quibbles over dogma and doctrines, I seemed to be trying to live a life that he could be proud of. I was not promiscuous, which was due both to my deep faith and my romantic ineptitude; I seemed to have overcome alcoholic temptations; I seemed to care about the poor; and had a relatively clean traffic record. Dad had taken notice, and I felt proud.

They made the move to Mission Viejo in south Orange County, and I dropped in every week, despite the crammed freeways that connect Los Angeles and Orange County.

I often sought to come just for lunch or dinner. Though they had promised repeatedly not to pressure me to visit them, their parental gene kicked in, and they couldn't help pestering me from time to time. They mastered the art of sounding slightly hurt if I had other plans on a particular weekend. And Dad felt that nothing short of a life-threatening ailment should prevent me from staying the night in a guest room.

"Why don't you stay the night?"

"Because traffic is fine now, but it'll stink during rush hour, Dad."

"So leave early tomorrow."

"But if I leave before you get up, what difference does it make if I stay over or don't? Just pretend that I'm staying over—it'll be the same result by the time you wake up."

"No, just stay over."

Of course, once I stayed over, they insisted that I stay for breakfast. And lunch.

I realized that the parental gene needs to care for a child, even after he turns 40 or 50 or 60. My staying over was deeply satisfying for my father—my sleeping under their roof made him feel that he was still providing for me, as did his efforts to cram food down my throat despite my dieting.

"Have some more chicken."

"I can't."

"Why not?"

"I'm already stuffed, it was delicious."
"So have a little more."
"No."
"What's wrong with you?"
"Look, Mom just told me I'm too fat, and you're now trying to feed me more?"
"Too fat? No. Have some more."
"Noooo, Dad!!"

Rockin' with the Lord, vaguely

Throughout my late 20s and 30s, I grew still more active at Hollywood Presbyterian. The church was filled with various saints of various ages, and I was proud to have friends praying for me who were in their 20s, 30s, 40s, 50s, on up through their 80s.

Frank and Jane Frankman were two septuagenarians who encouraged me and prayed for me. Sandra Mader was a sharp high-school principal who brought her savvy and liberal sensibility during our time together on the church governing board and the committee to find a new pastor, when the old one ran off to serve as chaplain to the U.S. Senate. Life was a series of committee meetings, stitched together by a warm sense of community. At many of these meetings (especially the missions meetings), grand old saints of the church prayed that my parents would come to faith in Jesus.

Not everyone was as unconditionally loving and community-minded as the New Testament may have commanded; but you had to admit that church was one of those rare places on the planet where strangers were likely to greet you with a warm welcome and a genuine concern for you and for the "fellowship of the saints."

Fellowship is not an unusual word in itself; but because it is an English translation for koinania, an ancient Greek term to describe the Biblical community, it was used to excess. It was even used as a verb, as in, "We'll be fellowshipping with coffee after the sermon ends."

We fellowshipped a great deal at summer and fall retreats, when we would head out to the mountains, dress like extremely white-bread people in our flannel shirts, and sing praise songs with our hands in the air.

Mom's brief and passing acquaintance with church led her to a conclusion on one occasion. "They seem to like to sing songs as a way of not getting bored, don't you think?"

"It's actually not that," I responded. "They say it's worship. Muslims silently pray a liturgical prayer on a prayer mat, but Christians say that they worship by singing."

"How can they think singing is worship?"

"I dunno. I guess they say that worship is adoration, and that you sing about the things that you adore and care about. That's why most songs are about romance, since people are obsessed with romantic love. So they say that, since they love God the most, they'll sing about God at church."

"Hmm."

"Yeah. I know. Anyway, that's what they say." Truth be told, I usually had mixed feelings about Christian worship. I rarely felt transported into the presence of God by singing the hokey and prissy contemporary praise songs that my peers enjoyed. I was attending church during an era in which churches were having major "worship wars," with older members strangling younger members for playing drums and saxophones during service, and with the youngest members demanding to throw out hymns in favor of a cheesy, soft-rock approach to worship music (and occasionally a harder, quasi-grunge approach).

As one who worshipped at the altar of Led Zeppelin and classic rock, I found such efforts to be watered-down blasphemies. And at least the more traditional Christian hymns had the sacred solemnity and gravitas that my Islamic upbringing favored anyway. And I wondered why contemporary Christian art in general was such weak sauce, given how accepting Jesus was supposed to make you alive in a way that no non-Christian was supposed to be. The pagans were having all the fun, and creating the best art, even though the Creator was supposed to be blessing the "other side." But the Christian praise band guys didn't seem blessed, they seemed gooey, sugary and wimpy—even the ones who tried to channel Kurt Cobain via the Holy Spirit.

Yet whether you were "praising the Lord" through contemporary pop or grand hymns or Islamic liturgy, the point of worship was to get beyond yourself and lose yourself within the grandeur of praising God. I admit that I never got as much out of this as I wanted (to which the good evangelical replies, "Well, grow up—worship is supposed to be about pleasing God, not you....").

I spent a great deal of time in the Fuller Seminary Library in Pasadena, reading Biblical commentaries in preparation for teaching Bible studies and BRICK classes. A main reason for heavy study was to avoid a scenario in which a class member would stump me with a theological or Biblical question. So I became well-versed in concepts such as kerygma, eschatology, soteriology, infralapsarianism and supralapsaranism, the Canons of Dordt, various creedal councils and what not.

I had always tended toward a bit of fanaticism, and I became fanatical about the particulars of theology. I and like-minded persons would move to a corner of the room at dinners and parties so that we could debate fine points of predestination, while less-obsessed church friends mocked us.

I used to dismiss them as wimps who lacked real passion for their faith. By contrast, as a Muslim who found Jesus, I felt like a spiritual Superman. I knew that Pauline theology did not allow for such boasts, so I did my best to keep my vanity between me and the good Lord.

III: The Gods Are Dead, or at Least Underachieving

Crazy for Jesus, or because of Jesus

I always recommended therapy for my crazier friends. I told them there was no shame in being crazy, and that I would never judge them for their craziness. Yet it was a devastating realization for me that I myself might be crazy enough to merit therapy. After all, I had read every self-help book around. I kept around a variety of psychologist friends, and I constantly processed my life with honesty. But I knew I needed to dig deeper into my psyche, to find out why I was struggling with bosses and authority figures, with women, and, well, with family.

Quite fatefully, my friends Tod Bolsinger and Steve Norris referred me to a brilliant psychologist named Jim MacCuish. "He'll be that strong father figure who'll challenge you to grow," Tod said. Steve agreed: "Don't go to a woman therapist, they'll just coddle you. Jim can really push you."

Actually, Jim was a psychiatrist, and that bothered me somewhat, because I felt I only needed a psychologist. He also called his clients "patients," which had me feeling even more defensive.

But the bearded, spectacled and avuncular man was perfect for the job. He knew when to call me out for behaving like an idiot, whereas with other people I could usually argue persuasively about how they were stupider than I. Most of all, he helped me trust my instincts. "Your instincts aren't infallible," he said. "But they're a better guide for you than analyzing everything obsessively." That may have been the best advice I ever got.

Jim wasn't nearly as dedicated a Christian as Tod and Steve thought he was, and I imagine they wouldn't have recommended him if they'd realized.

Jim helped us on our individual journeys of self-discovery, but he hardly had an agenda to have us all love the Lord. Sure, he helped Tod immensely as he grew into a senior pastor of his own church, and he helped Steve be a faithful elder at Hollywood Pres, but he also nurtured my own increasing desire to question how my doctrines and my experiences didn't add up.

Jim wasn't cheap—his rate was $200 for a 45-minute session—so I would occasionally ask him if we could move to a biweekly schedule. He usually told me without hesitation, "Geez, bad idea—I think you've got a long way to go." He was right, and I knew it.

CULTURAL COLLISION 11: The plane and skyscraper kind

Did September 11, 2001 change the world? Not as much as advertised. But it changed how Americans saw the world, and would later change how the rest of the world saw America.

Did 9/11 change me? Yes. It forced me to wrestle with who "my people" were. Were they Americans? Pakistanis? Peaceniks? Evangelicals?

That day, the phone rang at an ungodly hour. 6:42 a.m. No reason to answer the phone at that hour. It's probably a wrong number. Why waste all that effort for a wrong number?

When it rang again at 6:43 and 6:44, I realized it was no wrong number, but rather a concerted effort to ruin my day. My friend Tom, from BRICK, was on the line. "I'm really sorry, but I just had to talk to someone. A couple of planes flew into the World Trade Center. It's just awful."

I figured a couple of small propeller planes must have bonked the buildings, and wondered what the fuss was about. I flicked on the television as he talked, and saw the news coverage. Then I saw the footage of the second plane striking, and thought, geez, it's actually some kind of jet. It couldn't be an airline jet, though, could it? Isn't it just a small jet?

I watched more coverage throughout the morning, taking other calls from friends. I watched in a daze as the buildings fell. I shut off the television after a couple of hours, figuring that there was nothing I could do about the horror and that waiting for more information to trickle in wasn't making anything better. With the TV turned off, I realized that life seemed to go on. I went outside and listened to birds singing and watched the sun shining, and thought of how it was also shining way off in Argentina as women delivered babies and children went off to school and people lived their ordinary lives.

Sure, two buildings collapsed, and the Pentagon took a hit. But stuff happens, I mused in a typically unsentimental way. (Remember, I was the one who was oddly detached during the attack on our American school in Islamabad back in November of 1979). London and Berlin lost buildings every day during World War II. This hurts, but it shouldn't change us too much, I imagined. We had been insulated from the kinds of pain and horror that others face daily, and maybe now the insulation had been rent asunder. But it seemed everything else would stay mostly the same. The talking heads said that our daily lives would be altered drastically, but I wondered if, once Americans got annoyed by long lines at airports, they'd decide they could risk losing a couple of buildings every once in a while; but within a day, I realized how powerfully events had re-wired the psyches of hundreds of millions of persons.

I also pondered whether, if this did signal a transition, it signaled a deeper, longer transition. Not a short-term change in our daily lives but rather the slow decline of a Western civilization, the way every previous empire gradually fell. Barbarians helped polish off omnipotent Rome, and here the modern barbarians were beginning to make their presence felt. Fighting it, I felt, might be as futile as dead-bolting the door before the flood hits, or demanding another bag of peanuts as the airplane goes down.

On the evening of September 11, Ferhan called me in Burbank, California, and we both talked about the horror of it all while staring at our TV sets. "But boy," he said, "I just wish Americans could understand a little bit about how these sorts of things happen. I'm sure they won't be able to hear it, but sometimes their policies really do help make these things happen." He seemed to have a point, but I agreed few Americans would be able to hear it.

• • • • • • • •

Within days, it became clear that some people in the Middle East meant America great harm, and that America was going off to war as a response. But it was not immediately clear whether America was going to war against a small band of renegades or an ideology, or a religion, or a region. Mom and Dad stayed riveted to their TV in their Mission Viejo home. "Terrible, this is just terrible," Dad would repeat while pacing the family room. "People need to learn to understand one another."

The newspapers reported that an Indian man—who was not even Muslim—had been shot in Texas, and I found myself relieved that Mom and Dad did not live there anymore.

I myself felt squeamish. Marginalized, even. I felt as though Americans—whites, I mean—were going to hate us. By us, I mean anyone who looked Muslim. Here I was, a Presbyterian elder, but I sensed that hatred could be just around the corner.

In fact no one seemed to treat me differently. On September 12, a salesman at a Vans shoe store in Thousand Oaks showed so much attention to me that he seemed to be overcompensating, wanting his brown customer to feel at ease around him. I did not feel at ease, but I appreciated his effort. On a hot L.A. afternoon a few days later, I walked into a bank when an elderly woman asked me, "Why'd you bring this weather with you?" I smiled. I don't usually get that sort of comment, and I figured that Middle-Easterners were more on her mind than usual.

It took many days to begin to feel "normal" again in American society, and I spent much of that time hanging around Glendale, the neighboring community filled with Armenians who looked like me. Back in Michigan, Pakeeza began wearing a conservative Islamic scarf for the first time, in solidarity with Muslim women who had been harassed publicly. Given that she was 38 weeks pregnant by then, I told her she was being noble but silly for taking that kind of risk.

The national prayer service a few days later was magnificent, an ecumenical display of America's big-heartedness amidst uncertainty and sorrow.

By the 14th of September, Dad placed two small American flags in the rear windshield of his Mercedes. He placed an American flag on his front lawn. And he wore a flag pin on his suit coat. There was no doubt he was an American. "Terrible, this is completely terrible," he kept repeating while watching 9/11 coverage. "This terrorism is not Islam at all."

A few weeks later, Shabi managed to rise above his own dating foibles and get married.

Shabi and his bride Maria were putting on a $90,000 spectacle (just a tad more expensive than the flawless three-carat diamond ring Shabi had bought her) for 300 people at the brand new four-star St. Regis hotel near Laguna Beach.

To prophet or profit?

Though Mom and Dad had become almost comfortable with their apostate son, things changed one afternoon in the summer of 2002.

I had begun writing columns with the encouragement of two friends, Tom Provost and John Newcombe. Tom was a screenwriter from Port Arthur, Texas, and John was a writer and filmmaker from Chicago. Tom was a political junkie who read dozens of columns daily, and John helped develop new talent for his brother's L.A.-based Creators Syndicate.

Having spent my career as a publicist and ghostwriter for others, the time seemed right for me to start writing in my own name. Two years earlier, the *Japan Times* publisher, who was a trustee of USC, asked me if I wanted to audition for the role of a regular contributor. It seemed like the opportunity of a lifetime, but I did not have much to say. I wrote one piece about the political situation in Pakistan, then ran out of fresh ideas.

But after 9/11, I found I had many things to say, and more importantly, realized that people were interested in how my background intersected with the big things going on in the world—the rise of radical Islam, the immigrant experience and America, and what it generally meant to be a religious American in a secularizing nation. I also knew this kind of writing brought risks—like the risk of eventually being shot by religious fanatics who might not agree with me.

Here was my chance to be a pundit. But what kind of pundit? I studied the media for several months, looking at what role could be open for me. Fox News seemed to use brown-skinned experts who railed against the Middle East and demanded that it reform. I thought perhaps that could be my niche—the squeaky Pakistani wheel. Karey, a Texan belle at Hollywood Presbyterian, told me, "Rob, I think God has prepared you for just such a moment as this." It seemed plausible to me. I sensed great fame and great drama—and probably great headaches—on the horizon.

I imagined I could make big bucks with a book offering Americans, especially Christians, an introductory critique of Islam. But I worried that a Christian publisher would, in that environment, push me to write an inflammatory piece. If I was going to enter into the fray of religious discussions, with all the inter-family and intercultural headaches that would ensue, I wanted to pick my battles wisely and tastefully; I chose to hold off on writing a book. After a few visits by e-mail to the electronic doorstep of newspapers, the door flung open. The *Los Angeles Daily News* ran a piece from me in early July, and I was on my way.

I did far better in the first few months than I had a right to. It was a struggle for me to get opinion pieces published for relatively famous clients, but suddenly I was getting placements for my own pieces, even though I was obscure by comparison.

Less than a week after my debut as a pundit in the *Daily News*, the *Los Angeles Times* ran a piece by me, in which I controversially called for some "benign" racial profiling against folks like myself. I know, it seems crazy, but I feel it's better for people such as me to willingly approve of a few compromises than to let natural human xenophobia quietly build pressure and explode later.

The piece ran on a day on which Ferhan, Pakeeza and Emaan were visiting my parents in California, and Shabi and Maria dropped in for the occasion.

I showed the piece to Pakeeza. "Wow, you're famous!" she said. "I'm so proud of you!"

Shabi then looked briefly at it and shrugged.

Ferhan read it carefully and said, "It's a bit right-wing for my tastes." I then shrugged.

Then Dad sat and read it. I awaited his reaction. He handed the paper back to Pakeeza without comment.

I tried not to fish for comments, but couldn't resist. "So what did you think?"

He extended out his hand, parallel to the ground, and waved it as to indicate a so-so reaction. "It is… okay."

I bit my upper lip and acted as though I didn't care what he thought, but I knew this was a lie. I would never earn Acceptance from my father for my beliefs and expressions. He might accept me for having come out of his wife's womb, but not for what I felt was my life's calling. I acted as though this Acceptance from Dad didn't matter. But it did.

Writer gains minor fame, hijinks ensue

A bigger stir occurred one afternoon in early August of 2002. I had just woken up from one of the afternoon naps that are the unique privilege of freelancers and zoo animals, and lumbered over to check my e-mail when I noticed a note from Max Boot, then the editorial features editor of the *Wall Street Journal*, accepting one of my op-ed submissions.

My heart leapt. It seemed like a dream, or at least some unreal residue of my nap. If I could make it into the *Journal*, I reasoned, I would have arrived. I would be a different order of creature than other writers. The *Los Angeles Times* was nice, but it was not a national paper, no matter how much it wants to believe it is.

I barely slept the night the *Journal* article was posted on the web, worrying that something would go wrong. I woke up at 5 a.m. the next morning to get my hands on the printed edition, and drove around town looking for a place that carried it, which was harder than it seemed. Finally, a 7-11 cooperated, in perhaps an ethnic coincidence.

Entitled "Islam's Silent Majority" the article called on moderate Muslims to battle Islamic extremists for the sake of intracivilizational peace and the sake of their religion. As a way of holding up my own family members as examples of good, moderate Muslims, I mentioned in passing that they were able to accept me even though I had converted to some other, unnamed religion. I also praised my father for sinking his savings into a Pakistani school that would model something other than what the hate-filled madrasas did.

Not bad PR for the family, I thought.

I thought wrong.

I had suspected they might be queasy about it. After all, this was the first time I was outing myself as a non-Muslim in a major public forum. Although I had been doing it for years in small forums such as church lectures, this was the *Wall Street Journal*. So I'd planned on showing them the article that weekend, in person, using my best PR skills to help give context for why this article needed to be written and to help them see how they came out like heroes.

I didn't get the opportunity. Shabi called that morning, breathlessly. "Geez, is it true you made it into the *Wall Street Journal*? That's cool! A friend called me from Oregon to tell me."

He called Dad, who then called to ask me for the article, which ruined my chance to provide some crucial context, flattery and sweet-talking. I emailed him the article. An hour went by, with no response.

I called. Mom was first quietly grim, then angry. She growled about how I had stripped myself and them bare in front of the world. "You weren't supposed to tell anyone. I told you so many times not even to tell Pakeeza. And now you've told everyone."

"Mom, I know you told me not to tell Pakeeza—but I never agreed to that."

"Why do you have to go telling everyone?"

I can't hide everything that's important to me from other people. We were never going to be able to hide this stuff. It was going to come out."

"Well, you've ruined us."

"How? It's just the *Wall Street Journal*. Not that many people read it. A few eggheads... some business junkies."

"Well, now people will know that your father and I are bad people." Sobs encumbered her vowels and consonants.

"What do you mean?"

"If we had been good people, you wouldn't be the kind of person that you are." She hung up.

Shabi called soon after to say, "Look, I'm really proud of you but you know this stuff hurts Mom and Dad. Can't you write about something else—like maybe the Lakers?"

I told him no. I didn't have much else to say to him, nor he to me. I then left an urgent message for Ferhan, giving him a heads-up that Pakeeza may soon catch wind of some information about me that the family had wanted to protect her from.

Not having slept much, and now being accused again of destroying my family, I collapsed on my couch for a couple of hours. I awoke late that morning in a surreal fog. The room was spinning. The best day of my life professionally was now one of my worst personally.

Still, I didn't regret what I had done. I was not going to hide my beliefs or my commentary under a bushel. I went for a drive and ended up visiting the Ronald Reagan Library in Simi Valley for the first time, wandering around the place thinking, "Today I'm a contributor to one of America's great newspapers, but my life is hell."

It was my turn to grow angry. I decided to take a break from the family, not even calling Shabi or his wife Maria. If they were not sure they wanted me around, I was not sure I wanted them around. A couple of weeks later, Mom and Dad were forgiving and inviting. I ignored their calls and pouted.

Mom & me & the Boss

Shabi and Maria invited me to a Bruce Springsteen concert and I accepted—only to find that they had also invited Mom.

Who on earth takes his mother to a Bruce Springsteen concert? One does not expect to have a reunion with an estranged mother at a rock concert, yet there we were. We all met for dinner beforehand, which felt utterly awkward. Mom seemed gentle and conciliatory, like she missed me. I was still annoyed and hurt and ashamed for feeling that way.

The show couldn't have been short enough for me, even though I'm a Bruce fan. I grumbled under my breath, "C'mon, Bruce, wrap this show up. I don't want to be here." I rued my pettiness but maintained it nonetheless.

My old journalism adviser, Debra, with whom I still occasionally kept in touch, counseled me to have mercy on them, even though mercy no longer came easy. "It took them something like nine months to come around the last time you shocked them, remember? This time it took a couple of weeks. That's progress. Don't hold their feelings against them." She had my best interests in mind and spoke the truth accordingly. That allowed me to listen in a way that I would not listen to most people.

Is anything worse than apostasy?

Ferhan for his part was sympathetic about it all. He told my father that, though my article was painful, it was accurate about the problem and the prescription. He agreed it was time to lift the veil of my personal secrecy. We agreed I would come out to Ann Arbor and have the self-disclosure talk with Pakeeza.

I always got along famously with my first niece, Emaan; we seemed to connect within seconds of meeting each other. And I always felt that had something to do with the good vibe that I had with her mother and father. They would be excited to see me, and vice versa, and Emaan could pick up on the happy buzz.

But when I headed to Michigan that Labor Day weekend, I sensed the buzz would be different. The baby would not remember me, and my presence in their house would be painful, not joyful, this time.

Ferhan and Pakeeza picked me up at the Detroit airport and brought me back to their place, at almost midnight. They told me the baby would probably be up, because Pakeeza's sisters, who were visiting, wanted Emaan to be able to greet me. I walked to the front steps to the door and knocked. Pakeeza's sister Leila came to the door, holding little Emaan, who was now 11 months old. She looked adorable, wearing a cute little white outfit and a white beanie cap. I smiled at her. And she immediately smiled at me. She looked fascinated and delighted. And I have rarely ever been so touched in my life.

The next day, Ferhan, Pakeeza and I went to Barnes and Noble, ordered lattes and Italian sodas and danishes, then moved to a table. The moment was at hand, and I eased into my most articulate and smooth-talking mode.

"Well, Pakeeza. Um. Well. The truth is that I've, uh, had some differences with my family about religious issues. I, um, I, uh, I… I tend to have my own particular views that are hard to categorize in any easy way. It's all really quite complicated. I have real respect for your own views, but, well…." This muttering went on for a few minutes.

She finally interrupted my sputtering. "I know," she said. "Your mom told me last week that you're a Christian."

I furrowed my brow. Why would she make me go through all that rigamarole if she already knew? In a way, though, I was relieved. It showed she already knew yet still accepted me. My mind was racing to figure out which discussions we had had since she had heard, and felt comforted that she had not turned and ran.

"So how'd you react when you found out?" I asked.

"Oh. Well…. I already knew something strange was going on because of how your family was acting."

"Really?"

"So I figured you either had changed religions or you were gay…."

"Oh."

"….and I was really praying you were gay."

"Oh."

She admitted she was shocked when she found out. And that she was still shocked. "I don't care what anyone else thinks about your faith. I'm just worried about you," she said. "Because I intend to be in heaven, and I want to see you there too."

That is one of the classic lines that evangelical Christians use in badgering their own friends and family members to convert. Pakeeza had seemingly ripped a page from their book. She continued. "I'm sure I'm going to want to talk to you more about how or why you made that choice."

"Sounds great," I said. "Anytime."

"Um, be careful about taking him up on that offer, Pakeeza," my brother interjected matter-of-factly. "He can make your head spin."

In a way, it was a real compliment. "We think we know our stuff," he continued, "but he's no dummy. He knows more about the Quran than you do. So don't think you're going to chat him back into believing what you believe."

Through it all, Pakeeza clutched my brother's hand for comfort. "This is one of the hardest conversations I've ever had," she said. She and I had always had a lively relationship; we had always laughed and poked fun of one another and adored one another. Now I represented a huge boondoggle in her life.

We talked on and on. She said that Amber, one of her sisters, had seen an article in the *Wall Street Journal* by a "Robert Asghar" and had wondered if that was me.

"I told her it wasn't," Pakeeza said.

"Did she believe you?" I asked.

"Well, she said, 'But the writer made reference to some school in Pakistan that his Dad ran, just like Robbie. How many people like that could there be?' But I just said, 'Nope it's not him.'"

The next day, Pakeeza asked, "Do you really have to leave tomorrow, Robbie? Spend a few more days with us." I really couldn't but I was heartened by that. Had she made peace with it all? I don't think people in that position fully make peace with such things.

CULTURAL COLLISION 12: The Jihadist Christians

In the ensuing months, I began to notice a few developments:

Not as many people in churches and schools were interested in having someone like me discuss the differences between Islam and Christianity, or related topics such as the causes of political turmoil in the Arab world.

Despite how the Christian doctrines of original sin and universal human depravity should make believers too humble to break the world down into simple "we're good, they're evil" categories, American evangelicals as a whole indeed took such a binary approach in positioning fair-haired America against evil jihadists.

While I'd always believed Christianity to be a pacifistic approach to the world, my own Muslim family was far more pacifistic than American evangelicals. Polls showed evangelicals as being the most pro-war crowd in the nation. They saw all the conflicts in cosmic, good versus evil terms.

Dad, by contrast was a hippy peacenik, mumbling, "We need understanding and peace" whenever he watched the cable newscasts about war drums in Kabul and Baghdad.

All this shook the foundations of my faith. I'd always been something of a peacenik, going back to my years watching the *Gandhi* movie and lobbying for a nuclear freeze in the early 1980s.

How could I be following a "religion of peace" if so many people who were my so-called brothers in Christ wanted to bomb an "enemy" whom they did not understand?

I saw the sardonic bumper stickers asking "Who Would Jesus Bomb?" and I wondered if faith had no ability to affect some inherent human longing to find an enemy to oppose. (I'd later find that this inherent human longing is something called "coalition aggression," something Mother Nature placed in us to form close bonds with one group as we fight for survival against another group).

Christian friends shrugged and rationalized any failure on the part of Christians as part of sinful human nature.

I was able to understand, and had long argued, that our imperfect human nature meant that a person may not live up to Christianity's greatest ideals. But this was different. Too many non-Christians seemed to have healthy and enlightened views about reconciliation and forgiveness. It seemed as though one's religion had less to do with once "Christ-like" tendencies than one's natural temperament.

Salvation by Paxil

All the while, I felt a sense of letdown. Had God really done miraculous things in my life? With all those years spent at church, was I really any better for it than I was for having done therapy?

With Jim MacCuish's prodding, I had been on the antidepressant and anti-anxiety medication Paxil for a couple of years. And Paxil seemed to do more for my sense of peace than Jesus had. Paxil had done more to calm my insecurities and thicken my skin than Jesus did or prayer did or Bible study did. At that point, it was inevitable that I'd begin to drift, given how much my ties to the church represented an ongoing rift with my family.

• • • • • • • •

A little less than five decades after arriving in America, Dad seemed as though he could agree that life, as Shabi (and Robert Redford in *The Natural*) would say, "didn't turn out the way I'd planned."

We didn't live on the same street, or all drive the same model of car, and we were not all doctors, not all proper Muslims, and hadn't obeyed every command of our folks.

Mom changed too. She began life in America as a servile, dutiful wife, and later became, well, more American. Her legs always stayed covered, of course. She did not wear bathing suits at the beach. However, she came to believe that her life was not merely an extension of her husband's or kids', as exemplified when she returned to Pakistan to oversee the construction of the family's commercial property there.

Mom also insisted to Dad that they were a partnership, not a hierarchy, which was fine by him as long as she agreed with him. He complained when they could not agree, however. "Where did she get these ideas?" he asked. "I think she has been watching too much American TV. It has warped her brain." It was an ironic comment for someone who loved nothing better than to sit back with his family and watch *I Love Lucy* reruns. Still, "it has been a very good life," he would often say, despite all the odd twists in the road that we encountered. "We have been fortunate. It has been a lot of fun." Fascinating words from a man who said on his wedding night that he "didn't believe in fun."

By contrast, I think back to the fate of Altaf's father. Dad handled a far more difficult set of cultural setbacks with infinitely more aplomb and grace.

Dad also wasn't content to be a quiet, retired man. Much of that nest egg he spent so much time building (while neighboring American families racked up debt) went toward the construction and maintenance of a free school for village kids in Pakistan that I wrote about in the *Wall Street Journal*. He then began plotting the construction of the first of a series of universities for rural Pakistan, if he could only find additional resources. Few would help him.

What the world really needed: another blogger

I began blogging in earnest about political issues. A regular sparring partner was a guitarist named Dave, who somehow considered me a dear friend even though I mainly recalled him as my nemesis in my fruitless battle for the heart of a girl at church. September 11 had turned Dave from a Birkenstock-wearing liberal hippy to a Birkenstock-wearing neo-conservative hippy; and neither Dave nor I could change the other's mind. He insisted that Christ expected citizens of a free society to make tough moral decisions in the midst of a fallen world, and that such choices often involve the use of force to protect innocent lives.

I insisted that, while this was nice "secular" common sense, it wasn't in the spirit of the Bible's view of human depravity. In other words, an aggressive approach to securing the peace only decreases the peace within a fallen world. We think we're administering justice and charity through our troops, but others see our actions (with some justification) as an extension of past Western colonialism. I was always impressed, and saddened, by how politically conservative Christians could take Paul's admonitions about original sin to heart except in the area of patriotism. America was either perfect to them or so infinitely less sinful than other nations as to make humility or self-reflection a silly waste of time.

I took that as a betrayal of Christian principles. And I began to question where I stood.

I was flexible enough in my own Christian principles to begin driving around in a new BMW, even though that horrified some of my peers who felt that it's easier for a Hummer to squeeze into a compact parking space than for a luxury-car driver to get into the kingdom of heaven. The car was actually a gift from Shabi, who one day decided to put about $15,000 down to make the car payments affordable. They were affordable, but not cheap. Still, I felt as though I'd been transported to another dimension as I drove that 325 sedan.

What happened to all my lofty thoughts about the hard sayings of Jesus? What happened to the idea that a person must follow him to the end? I found myself reframing the issues. I began to see his statements as true enough expressions of how a person must be focused on higher principles at the cost of everything else. But I stopped viewing those statements as evidence that my life and the life of the Christian Church were inextricable. If there was a fellowship or communion of Christ-minded persons, that communion transcended the membership roll of church and in many cases replaced that membership roll.

I continued to write and get published in newspapers around the world: in Jamaica, Jakarta, Jordan and so on. I became a more-than-occasional contributor to the *Los Angeles Daily News* and *Charlotte Observer* and a few other papers. I was approached in 2003 by Eve Becker of Tribune Media Services, the newspaper syndicate in Chicago; she asked me to enter into a development agreement with them. It's like auditioning for a role in return for a small payment. I wrote phony articles for them for two months, which were read by Eve and by an editor named Bob Koehler, who would call me and pick them to pieces. He lamented my inability to get really personal and my tendency to stay in my head instead of letting my passions fly. After three months of paying me at the rate of $500 a month, they told me they'd run out of money but that they'd revisit my situation in six months.

I used the rejection as an opportunity to complete a draft of this book, and created a draft that received warm responses from people such as Tod, Tom and John.

Before those six months were up, I had gotten a call from Creators Syndicate, the group led by John's brother, Rick. They wanted me on board. I celebrated, alerted Eve by email (and got an icy congratulations note in response), and plotted imminent fame and fortune that soon grew un-imminent.

Freelance writing work became difficult, as assignments from the USC president's office and the engineering dean's office slowed to a trickle.

Bills felt more ominous than before. I knew I either needed to mount a campaign for new business… or get a day job. I remembered that Shabi had told me in 1999 that he'd happily take me on board as his personal writer for $100,000 a year—a huge increase over the $62,000 I made at USC. I'd never responded because I thought the sort of letter-writing he wanted was beneath me, but I was now hungrier and humbler.

Still, I was leery. He was my big brother, he could be quite prickly, and the idea of our working together posed some concerns. Nonetheless, my mother encouraged me to bring it up, thrilled at the prospect of two of her sons working together nearby. As we dined one night at our parents' place, I broached the subject.

"Hey, do you think you'd still want me to work for you?" I asked softly.

"Huh? For us?"

"Yeah."

"Doing what?"

"You know, you once mentioned me writing for you. Do you have a communications office? I could be a part of that."

"A communications office? Are you nuts? We're too busy doing our jobs to have a communications office."

"But every company has a communications office or a PR office."

"No they don't. Are you crazy? See, that's why you couldn't work with us. You don't know what we do or what we care about. You'd get killed in our business."

"Uh. Oh."

After he left an hour later, I looked at my mother and glowered. "Did you see that? That's why I'd never work for him!!!"

"I know. I know. I don't know why he treats you like a little brother. Or like an idiot." She was crestfallen.

A few days later, Shabi called to tell me he did want me to work for him. "How could that be?" I asked. He claimed he was being dismissive because he somehow thought I wasn't serious in intent. I suspect he also got a tongue-lashing from my mother.

I took the offer, and one early January night in 2004, I loaded up my car for the hour-long drive from Los Angeles to Orange County, where

I would begin work for Encore the next day. I felt a bit like a nomad, displaced again from my church home, which had become fractious and toxic in its politics. I hoped to make a new home.

I began renting a condo in a white-picket-fence townhome community in South Orange County, one that that Shabi and Maria owned and was close to them and to my parents. Mom loved having me just 15 minutes away, close enough for me to drop by for a home-cooked meal.

I was now a corporate communications officer making $90,000 a year plus benefits and bonuses at a fast-growing subprime company that had 600 employees nationwide. That figure would soon jump to 1,800, as the subprime and housing bubbles inflated. I was able to work with a radically new crowd—a bright crowd that worked hard and partied hard. They weren't the intellectuals with whom I dealt at USC or the Bible-study zealots of Hollywood. It was fun.

It was also a balm to have enough money to not brood over bounced checks. And it was refreshing, liberating, to get into the for-profit world—to work for a company that provided a simple service for a fee, without beating its chest about how it was enlightening minds or saving souls. The parties were also great, although I found myself wondering what to do around all the booze consumption.

A Christian friend at Encore ironically egged me on to resume drinking, despite my 17 years on the wagon. "You drank a lot in college," she said. "Here's a news flash—everyone in college drank a lot. I bet you could just have a social drink at a party without it being any big deal. You're not trying to impress people anymore with how much you can drink."

I sensed she was right, just as I'd sensed others were right who'd made that case over the years. My old, atheist roommate Jeff, who had told me that my Christianity was just a phase, had also told me to keep my party drinking in the perspective of my college phase of life.

In previous years, I'd claimed that I wasn't worried about the alcohol itself but was rather wanting to have a new chapter in my life. But now, it seemed that still another new chapter was beginning, and that it was time to attempt a social drink again. On Christmas night of 2004, which I spent with John Newcombe and his wife Frances, John offered me a glass of red wine, and I accepted it. I drank it without incident and without craving, and I woke up the next morning without repercussions. I was on my way to being an uneventful social drinker, and no unusual episodes occurred like in D.C. in my college days.

This fascinated me and liberated me further. I had always puzzled over America's odd relationship to alcohol. Most Pakistanis dreaded it, while a few hipsters secretly kept a stash. But America was schizo—it had party people mixed in with MADD prohibitionist types. Alcohol was a combustible issue in the Muslim world and in America (unlike Europe, where it was mostly just something that brought out the taste of your food).

A pagan again

A pastor friend in South Orange County, Morgan, asked me if I had found a new church community, and I said no. Morgan emphasized that he didn't want to meddle, but that he was concerned that I would find a community that could love me and support me and guide me. I understood this: A few years earlier, I tended to sneer when I saw peers "fall away" from regular church membership. "An unchurched Christian is a contradiction in terms," my mentor Tod often said. I had always agreed. But now, I agreed while being an unchurched Christian.

I was 39. I was tired of fifteen years of praying that God would bring me a wife who could be my ministry partner in reaching souls for Christ. I was tired of praying that God would touch my family's heart and turn them into Christians. I no longer had the heart to pray that I would remain a Christian.

Nothing that I encountered or thought was new to me. The events and musings that eroded my faith were the same things I had heard during my evangelical journey from "unbeliever" friends, the same arguments I had read in books. But they had a resonance, a verisimilitude, that they had previously lacked. I no longer bickered with these thoughts; I nestled with them. I entertained them on long commutes to the office, and on Sunday mornings while truant from church life.

Evangelicals would call that the work of the Devil, as he led me gradually astray through my doubts and through my isolation. Me, I was tired of hearing people claim the Devil was standing behind every curtain. I had always acknowledged the Devil as a vague sort of concept of evil personified, as a means of keeping the theological peace, but I never inhaled regarding the concept.

I also found myself reading Lao Tzu more frequently, that old friend to whom I ran in times of distress rather than to the Biblical writers. I found myself reading the Old Testament more closely, not for inspiration, but to look with clear eyes at how God supposedly called his people to kill "every living thing," even babies and animals, during the conquest of Canaan. (He did, however, tell them to save the fruit trees in the notorious Deuteronomy 20 chapter, since the trees would provide tasty fruit).

I found myself recognizing that even the most well-intentioned religion can be very vicious—and that, if some good-natured contemporary Jews and Christians could forgive and rationalize the Old Testament's savagery, they should be willing to understand how most ordinary Muslims weren't to be judged any more negatively for the violent acts of their extremists or the less friendly passages of the Quran.

• • • • • • •

Meanwhile, right-wing pundit Mark Steyn railed against the threat of high birthrates among Muslims in Europe. If a person had directed a quote like Steyn's toward Jews instead of Muslims, it would have been condemned as unforgivable racism. Why did my family deserve worse treatment? I felt enraged when Baptists like Steyn could say such vicious things about Muslims, while being celebrated by other conservative Christian pundits such as Hugh Hewitt.

Hewitt was a particularly onerous figure in my mind. Mark Roberts, a theologian who grew up in Hollywood Presbyterian, was his friend and pastor at a church in Irvine. Roberts and I engaged in some candid discussions about what I felt were heresies on Hewitt's part. Roberts claimed he could not publicly call out a member of his church, assured me that he'd shared his reservations in an appropriate private session, and pleaded for patience as "we're all works in progress, just like Hugh."

Roberts usually finessed the issue in this way, often while alternating between genuine concern and relative indifference, then asked something like, "So have you found a good church home that can nourish your spirit? I believe it's really crucial when writing about these hot political issues." I personally was flummoxed about what the point could possibly be of finding a church home; the American evangelical church, post-9/11, seemed to stand proudly against everything that I admired about its supposed architects, Jesus and Paul.

While living in Orange County, I found it harder to get to Jim Mac-Cuish's office for regular visits. When we did find time together, we would talk for two hours (while he only charged me for one) about the changes in my life, and about my gradual drift from a more rigid theological orthodoxy. Life felt as though it were softening, while becoming more real. I felt I was becoming more "present" in my own life. I admitted to him that I had abandoned evangelicalism, and he seemed to see that as progress.

Steve and Tod would have been crushed to find that the man who helped them so much in their Christian walk helped me leave my Christian walk. I don't think Jim (or I) would see that as a betrayal of principles. He helped each person down his own road. He wasn't there to pull Tod or Steve away from evangelicalism, nor was he there to push me back into it. As we became more like-minded, he allowed me more access into where he was coming from.

I began to spend more time reading science. As one who had ridiculed evolutionary biology in several newspapers, I now found myself suspecting that it explains better than any religious tradition the manner in which tribalism drives a decision-making process that is similar for pagans and Bible-lovers alike. I found myself mulling how temperament drives conduct more than Bible verses do—for example, when a pro-force, pro-power temperament overrides Jesus' words that Christians are not to view power and authority in the way that Gentiles do. Indeed, the manner in which tribalism and temperament seemed even more evident within the Christian church than outside it seemed to evidence evangelicalism's limited ability to live up to its claims of being the sole steward of absolute truth.

I also was enjoying a new sense of living freely. I could drive around town without a seatbelt and with a mischievous smirk on my face. I could have a beer once I got to my destination. I could ask out a woman who hadn't proved that she "loved the Lord," without feeling as though I was stepping into catastrophe. I could see that many non-Christians were having a pretty good time—a "blessed" time, you could say. I had spent so many years attempting to justify evangelical theology, by saying that the people who eschewed Church for Starbucks were poor saps who did not realize that they were lost in darkness and living death. And now I was spending Sundays at Starbucks, or at Diedrich's (which was the OC's improvement on Starbucks, until Howard Schulz predictably bought it out and crushed it).

My last Sunday as a church-going evangelical was at my friend Morgan's church in the posh community of San Juan Capistrano. Morgan and his wife Veronica had been close friends at Hollywood Pres. I sat next to Veronica and listened to him give a high-quality sermon on 1 Kings 18, in which Elijah and Yahweh get into a contest with rival priests of the god Baal. In the story, Baal fails utterly and Yahweh goes on to smite him handily. And afterward, adding insult to injury, Elijah has 450 of their priests massacred.

"The God who shows His strength in such a dramatic fashion will make His power available to you," Morgan said, "for the struggles and trials of your own life. He is present and He is powerful, for you here today."

I think my heart broke at that point.

God? He didn't seem any more present than Baal, and he certainly didn't seem more powerful. Did he really do a miracle in front of the Baal priests? It seemed all too convenient that all his miracles were done in times past, whereas anyone who noted that he was light on empirically falsifiable latter-day miracles was told that Jesus didn't think that you should look for a miraculous sign (even though his divinity was ostensibly proved by miracles). I was dizzy from it all. Religious apologists would say that past performance didn't guarantee future success; my view was that it was more sensible to see God's current performance as the best indicator of how he worked in the past. And the God that I saw at work then had little resemblance to the God of the Bible. He seemed a terrible underachiever, and I no longer felt it blasphemous to think such a thought.

He was supposed to be redeeming a world and making those who followed him capable of doing things they never could do without him. But the good things in the world, and the good people, just seemed to happen naturally, not with a noisy Yahweh pulling the strings.

My parents had never seen the Christian God do some Elijahesque display of power, no matter how much my churchmates and I prayed over fifteen years. Their Muslim faith was steady, and my Christian faith was buckling. Where was this powerful Christian God?

While my more irreverent church friends and I would make a salty comment about how we would imminently be struck by lightning for our naughtier comments or actions, I came to notice that he didn't actually strike anybody for anything—even though he allegedly struck people dead regularly in the Bible to provide a caution for the rest of us. When I heard evolutionary reasons explaining how religious commands arose from "heaven" as a way to encourage cooperation that was necessary to group survival, it began to ring more true to me than the idea that an actual Heavenly Being was meddling above.

I was angry at this underachieving God who was so much less than advertised, and I felt resentful about how I spent so much of my life as one of his advertisers. I was also seeing him as irrelevant. Irrelevant, perhaps, in the ways that classic Buddhists saw the notion of divinity as irrelevant to their working out of their destiny. Irrelevant, as even Dietrich Bonhoeffer seemed to see God as irrelevant to the life that a Christian must lead on his own strength. Either way, I was exhausted by all the efforts to contend that life can only be lived by relying on the miraculous strength of a God whose handiwork was obvious only in the pages of the Bible yet far harder to discern in modern life. I was exhausted by being stuck with people who believed that any happy coincidence or dramatic sign was a confirmation of God's goodness in their lives—and that any such sign was merely an act of Satan if it happened to an "unbeliever," be that a Muslim, new-ager, Buddhist or atheist.

I was tiring of the notion that Christ's goodness was exclusive to those "in the kingdom." I grew tired of believing that the people who attended church on Sundays were "new creations," to use Paul's term—even though that once gave me a sense of purpose (and perhaps superiority) on Sunday mornings, as I passed by the pagan flocks reading the *L.A. Times* on Sunday morning at Starbucks while I dutifully took my latte to church.

I grew tired of believing that my church pewmates were "alive" in Christ, while those still at Starbucks were "in death," as supposedly were my growing brood of nieces and nephews. Tired of believing they were distinctly different from Hindus or Muslims, when they just seemed to be nice people who would embrace whatever religion happened to prevail where they were born and raised. God bless the evangelicals, but I didn't feel as though I could be a part of them anymore.

I woke up the next Sunday morning and felt an odd feeling. I came to a realization —a recognition that I was no longer an evangelical. I had "lost faith," as they say. And I felt great. I felt exhilarated and liberated.

I celebrated by driving up from Ladera Ranch to the Bodhi Tree Bookstore, that anarchic orgy of spirituality on L.A.'s Melrose Avenue. I also began to take up science, especially evolution, finding a sense of humor in how the human animal isn't much different from its chimpanzee peers. I began to open up about this to those evangelical friends who could stand it.

• • • • • • •

What happened to my "gift of faith," as evangelicals would call it? I don't know if it's a gift per se. Religion does seem to play a vital role for the human animal—providing "necessary delusions" that enable someone to generate hope for the future, strength for the present, and peace about the past. I just felt that I would be finding that hope, strength and peace from other means, which I came to believe existed in great quantity.

Pastor Greg Boyd, in *The Myth of a Christian Nation,* tells the story of a pious woman who was about to be sexually assaulted. In her moment of despair, out of nowhere, some compassionate words came to her. "Your mother forgives you," she said to her assailant. He broke down in tears. Having spent years victimizing women after having in some way violated his own mother as a teen, he kept sobbing till the cops arrived, and later thanked the woman for helping him find God. The woman also might have escaped if she had a gun, but she wouldn't have made a better world in the process. That story showed the best within the Christian tradition, and I wondered why Christians lost sight of such lessons when it really counted—like when wars were on the horizon.

When the war broke out in Iraq, my Muslim family viewed it with great skepticism, less convinced that it was an act of compassionate liberation and more convinced that it was as a John-Waynesque act of old-fashioned butt-kicking against a Muslim nation. This belief was fueled by the fact that the U.S. used kid gloves with a North Korean nation that seemed to pose a more imminent threat of obtaining nuclear weapons. This belief was fueled too by George Bush's openness about how his governance was driven by his evangelical faith, and because he said he was on a "crusade," using a term that Muslims associate with massive slaughters of Muslims and Jews in past centuries. When we think of how blacks cringe when they see confederate flags waved by white Southerners, we should remember that Muslims grow up with a similar reaction to the crusades.

As big a Bush critic as I was, I spent countless hours trying to convince them that the war was not a war against Islam. I told them that it was an ill-considered and naïve attempt to bring peace to the Middle East, but I insisted it was neither an attack on Islam nor an oil grab.

I worried over the various readers of *Little Green Footballs* and *FrontPage* who believe that Muslims are a vicious race that can't be reformed. They were joined by eight million listeners of Michael Savage, who called for the killing of 100 million Muslims. And by frustrated war supporters whose emails to me hit much harder than they did a couple of years ago, calling me a "sick individual" and a "traitorous member of the Muslim enemy." (Even a mainstream conservative such as Rich Lowry or a congressman and presidential candidate such as Tom Tancredo mused that nuking Mecca could be a good move).

Later I wondered if my parents might have been right. Maybe it really was a war against Muslims after all. I knew that most of my conservative buddies weren't fighting a war against Islam, but most of their unseen allies in the war were. Did that not bother them at all? Did it not show anew why the New Testament had a certain wisdom in its admonition that repaying evil with evil makes situations deteriorate further?

I had first become interested in Jesus' call for unconditional and redeeming love through the new-age guru Marianne Williamson, before I became involved with an evangelical movement that condemned her as a heretic. It was fascinating later to see Williamson lobbying for a U.S. Department of Peace that would equip people with conflict-resolution and cultural-understanding skills. I felt I'd take her heterodoxy over orthodoxy anytime.

Some good news and bad news

One night, while Dad was in Pakistan, working on his charity project, I dropped by their house for dinner with mom. We made small talk about the peculiarities of subprime mortgages, and then I offered a couple of revelations: "So I've started doing social drinking again. And, um, I've stopped going to church."

"What?" She grew grim and urgent. "But Robbie. Didn't you have problems with drinking? Why...?"

"You know, I thought about it for a lot of years. Some pretty sensible people told me that I didn't have any unusual kind of problem, and that I was drinking a lot in college, just like everyone else. Being out of college, there wouldn't be that same pressure to drink too much..."

"But..."

"...So I just don't think it's that big of a deal. And it hasn't been. It's fine. I like having a social drink with people, and not making a big deal out of it one way or the other. I just don't see the need to go to extremes about it in either direction."

She looked unconvinced, and of course you'll never convince a dedicated Muslim that it's ever a good idea to have a beer. But she then paused, raised an eyebrow and asked, "So what about this other thing? What do you mean you're not going to church?"

"I'm sick of all this, Mom. I'm sick of all the arguments between people who think their way of thinking about God is the only way. I'm tired of all the labels about what I should be called and I'm tired of all the different camps. I'm not going to walk around anymore claiming that my camp is the only one that's right, or that everyone else is wrong. I'm just tired of it."

She paused, them moved forward to embrace me. She began to weep. She said, "I've been praying, 'God, please let him see that we're not so different." A divide crumbled.

A few minutes later, she gathered back her composure and sat at the dining table. "Well, now I can start looking for a wife for you again."

Some things never change.

BOOK 2

Lessons from the Holy Wars

I. Lessons from the Department of Homeland Insecurities

Immigrants will catch the "America bug" without even realizing it
Mom and Dad figured they would spend "just a few years" in America because of the job opportunities here. Then they'd return to Pakistan with a little extra cash and bring their kids up there the way kids there had been brought up for centuries. But they took on more of America than they had bargained for. They caught something called the "America bug."

The "America bug," a sort of mad-cow disease for immigrants, was first described to me by Steve Sample, the USC president, who noticed that foreign students tend to catch a cultural infection here that bends their plans and alters their dreams. If they return to their homeland, they wish it was more like America, and will work to make it so. Often they choose not to go home, or choose to return to America after a while.

Once infected, you begin to see life in a cockeyed manner; you begin to believe you can write the script of your own life instead of letting family or culture write it for you; you fume on your visits back home that life is too corrupt or inefficient or boring; and while you're concerned about the feckless morality of America, you also sense that these Americans aren't overly uptight, and something feels right about that.

And when your children begin to drift from your heritage, as was the case with Ali's progeny, you may stay awake late cursing this place, but you suspect your destiny is tied inextricably with it.

Europeans spilled blood over issues of morality, papal authority and the nature of the bread served during Communion; this helps explain why they now flinch when God is even mentioned.

In the case of Christendom, what finally freed up the best in religious thought and deed? The America bug did. The New World bespoke life, liberty and the pursuit of the good life. Americans were willing to fight to the death for justice, but not over private matters of conscience.

Similarly, the America bug is what might slowly kill off the fanatic appendages of latter-day Islam.

America, stunningly, has gone eight years now without a major terrorist incident on our soil. This may be due to luck, prayer and outstanding work on the part of our government workers; but there's another reason that would-be terrorists have failed to make a dent here since that black September day. "A lot of these guys lose the jihadi, desert spirit," an intelligence agent told *Newsweek*. "They get families, they get jobs and they lose the fire in the belly. Welcome to America."

Welcome, indeed.

Mom and Dad rued that Shabi and I grew up much less Pakistani than they'd hoped, but they made peace with it.

Still, they tried another strategy with Ferhan, sending him to Islamabad to learn the right values. In an eerie recapitulation of my father's story, he came to the U.S. for a medical education, and later brought back a wife from an arranged marriage in Pakistan, hoping to spend "a few years" building a career, and well, you know the drill.

He and Pakeeza have sensed they're here to stay. They hear me talk about the idea of an America bug and they nod. They caught it, or it caught them. Barring an increase in anti-Muslim sentiment (perhaps if our luck runs out and there's another major attack) they'll be here.

Their daughters Emaan and Zara may be the future of Islam. The willful urchins will someday bicker with their mom and dad over whether they need to observe halal (the Muslim version of kosher) food standards. Now they are fans of floral dresses, but they may one day question or even protest their parents' disdain for skirts at parties or shorts in gym class.

Their parents may wonder why they didn't whisk the girls back to Pakistan when they had the chance. And then, like my father before them, they'll remember the confounded America bug.

After navigating those icebergs, they will find that America changed their approach to life, just as it has changed everything else it has touched. They will see that America gave their faith the slack and the context it needed to adapt to a new era.

They will be grateful for America, and so, hopefully, will our world.

Immigrants can re-teach Americans some personal discipline— but we should still draw the line at Shake 'n Bake

Perhaps all my parents' fasting during the holy month of Ramadan made it easier for them to live lives of self-restraint. But some of that self-restraint seems common among immigrants, which is nice to remember in an era of backlash against immigration. (Don't the native Americans wish they'd been as stringent in immigrant standards as today's talk-show radio crowd...?)

Mom and Dad long sensed their American neighbors were addicted to splurging—even back when Americans saved a dime on every dollar in the 1980s and a nickel on every dollar in the 1990s, well before the national savings rate went negative in 2005 for the first time since the Great Depression.

"It's not all about *fun*," they'd say in response to my nagging questions about why we couldn't keep up with the Joneses and their long vacations, fancy cars and new gadgets. We were the last people on our street to get a color TV or a microwave oven, even though Dad was an accomplished electrical engineer. Mom and Dad reflected in their lives that centuries-old pattern of immigrants arriving in this nation with a grim resolve to improve their family's future, playing the role of industrious ants to Aesop's consumerist grasshopper.

As an adult, I believe that sort of approach has a lot going for it in a nation that now owes $1 trillion to China and $13 trillion (and climbing) to a variety of other interests. But as a child, that approach annoyed the pee out of me. On our occasional trips to the Kings Dominion amusement park in Virginia, we would enjoy various roller coasters; we would walk past the delicious, aromatic hamburger stands... and we would walk back to our car, where mom had prepared for us a large supply of Shake 'n Bake chicken. It was supposed to be as good as the Colonel's Fried Chicken, but it wasn't. It was mild, and boring… and cheap.

My parents always bragged about our nest egg. Why not spend a few bucks on burgers at Kings Dominion, I wondered? Yet they believed that it was precisely their approach to savings that gave us a nest egg in the first place.

Turned loose as an adult, I made it a point to rarely cook. It was a hollow and costly rebellion, but I was determined to eat out three times for every one time our family went on the cheap. I've almost achieved my goal. But beyond my willful overspending, I admire the ant more than the grasshopper, and I think our immigrants have something to teach each new American generation about the way of the ant.

A good devil can bring peace

We like war—there's no way around it. Whether we're fighting land wars or culture wars, and whether we're using bombs or words to destroy others' lives and chosen identities, we prefer to wake up to enroll in a holy cause against "those devils out there" than to reconcile with jerks or to compromise some aspect of our own identity. It may be high time for progressives to think differently—and more practically—about peace, based on the increasing evidence that human beings are *built* for war.

Within the Mideast, the biggest obstacles to peace are angry beehives on both sides who believe that compromise equals defeat, and who won't soon be convinced that conciliation pleases the gods. Jerusalem can't be split, Palestinians must have the right of return, settlements must be abandoned, and so on. Peace involves un-ringing a series of bells. Good luck with that.

The Mideast remains the quintessential territorial contest, which Harvard evolutionary biologist E. O. Wilson boils down to this reality:

> [I]ndividuals hereditarily predisposed to defend private resources for themselves and their social group pass more genes on to the next generation. Humanity is decidedly a territorial species. Since the control of limiting resources has been a matter of life and death through millennia

of evolutionary time, territorial aggression is widespread and reaction to it often murderous. It is comforting to say that war, being cultural in origin can be avoided. Unfortunately, that bit of conventional wisdom is only a half truth. It is more nearly correct—and far more prudent—to say that war arises from both genes and culture and can best be avoided by a thorough understanding of the manner in which these two modes of heredity interact within different historical contexts.

Mother Nature seems to have decided long ago that our survival as a species requires a mix of collaboration and competition—collaboration within a social group, competition to protect territory from rival groups. Six billion people later, it's hard to bicker with her reasoning. The approach has been labeled coalition aggression, a trait especially common among men, according to Rose McDermott, a Stanford University political scientist. (Indeed, studies show that male college students will be more generous than female students in raising money for charity, *if* the financial request is framed as a battle against a rival school).

What's the implication for foreign policy? Consider the famous words of my hero, Eric Hoffer: "Mass movements can rise and spread without belief in a God, but never without belief in a devil." Effective foreign policy requires effective diplomacy that helps frame devils productively and proactively.

This is where pragmatism comes in. The human species may someday evolve to the point where we can sell majorities on the warm fuzzies that come from compromise and hand-holding, but we're not there yet.

Take Pakistan as a devil-management case study. For decades, civilian and military leaders have managed public attention by rallying them against some "imminent" plan on India's part to take Pakistan over. My Indian friends insist that they wouldn't want Pakistan or know what to do with it. Just the same, enough woofing comes from across the Indian border to make the Pakistani public believe that the Indians are a greater devil than their own incompetent government.

A new coalition of civilian leaders, led by people such as Pakistani-American rock star Salman Ahmad, has been revving up reform movements within Pakistan. Ahmad launched *Hai Hamara!* (Pakistan Is

Ours!), based on an old feel-good sports anthem by his band, Junoon. "This place is *ours*, dammit!" is a good strategy to rally a beleaguered people to take back their destiny from a meddling Taliban and from a corrupt political process. It takes the emphasis off foreign devils—not just India, but an America that has been viewed with so much distrust that the Taliban often has seemed like a useful foil. It puts the emphasis back on matters of which Pakistanis can feel competitive pride in taking ownership. (Don't minimize the gains from spurring a people's pride and competitiveness—especially in shame-and-honor based cultures).

We may well achieve a post-territorial, post-war mentality. We appear not to have evolved much physically in 100,000 years. But for the past 30,000 years we have begun evolving culturally at a fast clip. And in recent centuries, we may be evolving morally, increasingly rejecting such staples of homo sapiens as slavery and genocide.

But we can't get ahead of ourselves. To engage citizenries productively in the short term, we'll have to find demons that are both compelling and manageable.

Soldiers, pirates, vampires and terrorists all have something in common

Dad often fumed about how George Bush was an evil man, even a religious fanatic. I'd tell him, "C'mon, Dad George Bush strikes me as a nice guy who just feels his family is under threat from the neighbors, and who deals with it in a clumsy way."

I felt the mistake Bush made was that he declared war not on specific neighbors who meant him harm, but on an entire category of violence—terrorism. This was a messy and even hypocritical strategy, since one man's terrorist is another man's freedom fighter, and since most civilized societies have been able to accommodate some form of terror when it suited their interests. The English even gave commissions to pirates—the terrorists of a past age—when they proved helpful in tormenting the government's Spanish rivals. Similarly, many American policymakers applauded fanatical Arab Muslim terrorists, as long as their rage was focused against "godless communists." In his Pulitzer-winning book, *Ghost Wars* (which is must reading for anyone who seeks to understand the political and historical relationship between the U.S. and "Af-Pak"), Steve Coll noted that one secular Afghan prophetically warned short-sighted Americans and Saudis during the Soviet occupation of Afghanistan, "For God's sake, you're financing your own assassins."

Inevitably that very brand of jihadist became the target of a "crusade" against evil in the minds of President Bush and neoconservatives after 9/11. But did those crazy Wahabi hillbillies "hate freedom" any more *after* the end of the Cold War than they did before? No, they just started being a threat instead of an asset. And some bitter Arabs and South Asians kinda got a kick out of seeing the mighty U.S. suddenly terrified, which is the whole point of terrorism.

Yet should Americans be so stunned that such persons could create t-shirts with the image of a mass murderer like bin Laden?

If we're committed to genuine understanding—and let's concede that most people aren't—then we need to remember Americans' own pop-culture fascination with outlaws and vigilantes. With pirates. With Vikings. With vampires of both the teen and adult variety. With various rogues that we romanticize and that we dress up as on Halloween. Pirates rape and steal and kill, but we somehow distance ourselves from the unpleasantness and instead create charming images of Captain Jack Sparrow. We find ourselves somehow seduced by notions of pirates and teen vampires who serve only their own interests—yet jihadists are often able convince an ordinary Muslims that they're fighting on his behalf against a Western world that cares only for oil supplies and Israeli domination, not for suffering Palestinians or innocent victims of American bombings. How precisely do we manage to romanticize some vigilante images while being so shocked by the catharsis that some post-colonial citizenries feel when they see us get kicked in the teeth?

As for the fact that terrorists are vile because they kill innocents, think of how we view soldiers who are "legitimate" instruments of war. We never forgive a foreign soldier for killing our innocents, but we romanticize and glorify our own soldiers for their almost Christ-like sacrifice—no matter how many innocents they may have killed on the other side. So more moral consistency would help as we go forward.

We could even consider the example offered by St. Augustine, who told the story of a pirate who met Alexander the Great and who informed Alexander that they were less different than it seemed: "I've got just one ship, so you call me a thug. You've got a whole fleet, so you call yourself emperor." Those of us who live in powerful empires don't like to hear that sort of perspective—but it's unfortunate that such wisdom is so easily dismissed by American Christians who claim to follow Augustine's example.

For their own sake, Arabs and South Asians desperately need to get over their feeling of victimization. But for our own sake, demonizing frustrated Arabs for their romantic fascination with contemporary rogues doesn't make for better relations; truly addressing the frustration makes things better. That "public-diplomacy" approach was ridiculed by the Cheney crowd, but their own approach hardly scared off those who would threaten us.

Look a little more closely at how a neoconservative and a jihadist both seek to stoke the flames of a cosmic conflagration, and you can see that they are unconsciously allied. Each is fighting for power against the moderates and progressives within his own society, each is jealously claiming to be the only worthy protector of his society, and each desperately needs the other as a perpetual foil. Cheney and bin Laden owed much to each other, and each would have had diminished relevance without the other.

But the rest of us don't have to be their suckers.

Hawks fear "shrink"-age

Conservative and hawkish pundits were twittering—again in the pre-technological sense of the word—about President Obama's "global apology tours" early in his term.

It is inappropriate for a president to act decently toward leaders of other nations, they charged. Does he seriously think America will be rewarded for bringing good manners and good hygiene to global gatherings? Does this callow fool not understand that America must play a ruthless Moe to the planet's other stooges?

These experts' main achievement has been to betray an unfamiliarity with human nature and with that touchy-feely psychology thing that they so fear.

A German-born foreign-policy expert at Stanford's Hoover Institution, best captured the hawk zeitgeist in a *Wall Street Journal* op-ed, which he concluded thusly:

> Conflict between states is made from sterner stuff than bad manners or bad vibes, past grievances or imaginary fears. International politics is neither psychiatry nor a set of "see me, feel me" encounter sessions. It is about power and position, about preventing injury and protecting interests. Love and friendship move people, not nations.

Could it be true that "love and friendship move people, not nations"? Hardly. What works at the individual level is just as likely to work at the collective level, and what fails at the collective level is just as likely to fail at the individual level.

When it comes to the United States' relationship with Israel, it is most decidedly about love and friendship; otherwise we'd have tossed the relationship long ago in favor of Arab oil. And this love and friendship represents a recent psychological shift, driven in part by conservative American Christians who now value traditional nation-state interests less than the ability of Jesus to return soon to a Netanyahu-governed Jerusalem.

Love and friendship, not simply a cold and calculating sense of self-interest or national interest, are what bound Tony Blair to George Bush, as Blair towed his unwilling nation behind him.

Look at the flip side. Mean words, not sticks and stones, are why many have viewed men such as Hugo Chavez and Mahmoud Ahmedinejad as threats. But American hawks should have more interest in those leaders' natural resources and geopolitical influence than in their posturings, which means that hawks are far more vulnerable to psychology than they realize.

Chavez called the haughty Bush a devil, and hawks decided he's an enemy. Chavez got some nice photo ops with Obama, and hawks derided

Obama as a wimp. A more mature approach is to understand that, just as we would demonize Chavez less if he stopped calling us devils, other nations would hate us less if we stopped treating them and their leaders like fools.

So I would challenge the words of the Hoover Institution fellow by saying something like this:

> The way the last superpower chooses to bestride the world brings with it hard consequences. Does the United States open its arms or ball up its fists? Growling rarely elicits smiles, and distrust never reaps its opposite. To present a friendly face to the world is not a matter of saccharine niceness but of well-considered interests, especially for a fearsome giant like the United States. For trust breeds authority, and authority breeds influence.

But here's a twist. This rebuttal is a word-for-word quote of another column *by* that same Hoover fellow, from May 2008. That column ran in the *Washington Post*, which is a bit less bellicose than the *Journal* and which was willing to run his sunnier side.

What explains the difference in his more recent hawkish views and the previous year's "friendly face" views? As a writer for the *Huffington Post*, I figured it was only right to ask the guy directly. Contacted at his Hoover Institution office, he wrote back to say that I quoted his 2008 *Washington Post* piece "a bit out of context," insisting that he was writing not about foreign policy in the *Post* but about encouraging American bureaucracies, post 9/11, to be more welcoming to foreign visitors.

I felt I could concede that. Yet his comment about how trust breeds authority, and authority breeds influence, shows that even he can see that love and friendship can move nations.

Further, "bad manners or bad vibes, past grievances or imaginary fears," at which he rolled his eyes in his *WSJ* piece, also move nations: Nuclear-tipped Pakistan and India are forever moving one another based on past grievances and imaginary fears and bad manners. Pakistan holds its status as "the world's most dangerous place" precisely because of imaginary fears that India and others have done nothing to allay.

It may not be fair to call this Hoover Institution fellow, a critic of the Iraq war, an outright "hawk." But like many war-fans and like most Obama critics, he struggled to make sense of human behavior, at either the individual or collective level.

The dismissiveness of "soft power" by hawks reveals, like a slip, their belief that dialogue and understanding are for sissies, and that the manner of civil and mutually enlightening discourse that harks back to Pericles is merely an obstacle on the course of aggressive action.

Oddly, many hawks claimed that we'll need another generation to see the value of Bush's Lone Ranger approach, yet they didn't need more than a few weeks to dismiss Obama as a wimp who had too many "see me, feel me encounters" in college.

But move from the touchy-feely realm of therapy to the more empirical, hardnosed realm of evolutionary psychology, and you see anew how the human brain's reptilian stem is hard-wired to choose enemies, especially at the tribal or national level, based on simple impulses of fight or flight. An American president who doesn't act like a jerk gives fewer reasons for foreign publics or leaders to mobilize against us.

As Americans attempt to decide whether to cajole or crush the world, the detractors of Obama's "global apology approach" remind me how dangerous a false toughness can be. But I'm always happy to sign up such persons for the next available "see me, feel me" encounter with my friend Jim MacCuish.

Most people's—and states'—attempts to become more secure seem to lead to their becoming less secure

Dad and Mom were technically born in India. Pakistan was created out of the ribs of India during the sweltering summer of 1947, after Britain ceded rule of the area. Pakistan is the result of India's Muslims feeling that they couldn't be safe, after the British left, amidst their Hindu rivals.

Given that the nation's Muslims were concentrated in the east and west regions, those regions were designated East and West Pakistan. East Pakistan broke away in 1971, with the aid of a still-bitter India, and became Bangladesh. West Pakistan became plain old Pakistan.

Why did Pakistan go on to become what news magazine covers labeled "The Most Dangerous Place in the World"? Most of it had to do with the ongoing rivalry with India. Most of it had to do with a perception that Pakistanis weren't safe from Indian bullying. That ultimately led to much of the world feeling threatened by Pakistan.

It was because India had nukes that Pakistan insisted on having nukes, even, as former Prime Minister Zulfakar Ali Bhutto (Benazir's father) said, "if we have to eat grass." Thanks in part to punitive sanctions by Washington, some of them did have to eat grass, and many in that country have long memories of how Washington seemed unfairly to keep them from matching India's nuclear prowess.

It was because India seemed to be a threat that some Pakistani military and intelligence officials found mujahideen-spawned forces such as the Taliban to be useful longer than the CIA did. Those jihadist forces could harass India and could also be a more useful anti-Indian presence on Pakistan's western border than guys like Hamid Karzai.

In short, Pakistanis' fear of India is why Pakistan has some 80 nuclear weapons and some crazy jihadists who'd love to get their hands on them.

Americans for our part, wanted to be safe from communism. But our leaders never did the math on what would happen later when a well-mobilized and equipped mujahideen would need new targets to keep their rage occupied. Combine that short-sighted decision with a selfish refusal to help the Afghans rebuild (we left it to the Pakistanis, who as I just noted, had their own agenda). The result is that both America and Pakistan are less safe than we were immediately after the dissolution of the communist bloc.

To understand Pakistani anti-Americanism, think of Pakistan as Washington's jilted lover

Hell hath no fury like a scorned ally. Pakistanis feel they gained nothing for aligning with America during the Cold War while India aligned with the Soviets. Toward the end of the Bush Administration, Washington sought nuclear cooperation with India; yet Pakistanis remember the damaging sanctions that Washington imposed on Pakistan in recent years for merely seeking to match India's nuclear capacity. Being rejected as a lover is one thing; being jilted for your greatest rival is more than most countries can take.

Here's another reason for Pakistani resentment of the U.S.: After 9/11, many Pakistanis saw the West as the plush, gated community adjacent to Pakistan's barrio. Some dramatic break-ins from barrio residents compelled the gated residents to demand that the barrio clean itself up immediately. The barrio residents wearily argued that they cannot fix matters so easily—and besides, they are more exposed, daily, to the threat of their own worst citizens than are their neighbors in the gated community.

In past eras Washington would forgive Pakistan's failures in democracy whenever forgiveness served short-term American purposes—say, while enlisting Pakistan's help in wars in Afghanistan against communists or terrorists, or while maintaining Pakistan as a cold war bulwark while neighboring India aligned itself with the Soviet Union. But whenever the American need for Pakistan has been less urgent, Washington often punished Pakistan through neglect or ponderous sanctions.

Poverty claims nearly half of Pakistan's 175 million citizens, and religious extremism has its own claim. Pakistan's own leaders balance worthy goals with a corrupted government machinery and hard-core religious elements. Former president and general Pervez Musharraf walked a highwire, and for his trouble he endured two assassination attempts in rapid succession.

For our part, we as Americans need to recognize the difference between aiding a citizenry and aiding a particular regime. Sanctions against Pakistan failed to deter its leaders from developing nuclear weapons in the 1990s, but did help alienate generations of ordinary Pakistanis.

The great Roman philosopher Seneca believed it was better to ignore slights—words that my father lived out in segregation-era North Carolina; Pakistanis tend not to let go of grievances easily. That leads to our next lesson.

When visiting Pakistan, expect no subtlety

I sat in on a meeting in August 2009 with Judith McHale, the State Department's new Undersecretary for Public Diplomacy, with a special charge to rebuild America's image in the Muslim world, especially in places such as Pakistan. A successful Pakistani businessman assured Undersecretary McHale, who was about to make her first visit to Pakistan, that she would find the majority of Pakistan's population to be moderate and friendly, despite polling data reporting that some 60% of Pakistanis saw the U.S. as the greatest threat to their nation.

McHale went on to meet with a range of Pakistani leaders and civilians, including Pakistani journalist and drama queen Ansar Abbasi. As the *New York Times* reported:

> After Ms. McHale, the Obama administration's new under secretary of state for public diplomacy and public affairs, gave her initial polite presentation about building bridges between America and the Muslim world, Mr. Abbasi thanked her politely for meeting with him. Then he told her that he hated her.
>
> "'You should know that we hate all Americans,'" Ms. McHale said Mr. Abbasi told her. "From the bottom of our souls, we hate you.'"

Gosh, no, Mr. Abbasi. Thank you for *your* time. McHale's willingness to meet with openly anti-American politicians and journalists such as Abbasi (who had applauded Iranian President Mahmoud Ahmedinejad as the exemplar for a Muslim leader) showed she was bold enough to tap a beehive in search of honey.

Yet I found myself pondering the vast difference in perspectives the businessman and the journalist offered McHale regarding Pakistani sentiment.

The amateur psychologist within me finds Pakistani society on the whole to be a bit bipolar. (Bear in mind, I say this with all due clinical non-judgmentalism). As that nuclear-armed, poverty-smitten nation hovers on the brink, its populace swings wildly between outlandish, outsized expressions of rage and despair on one end, and on the other end soothing if disingenuous assurances that life in Pakistan, like a work of modern art, isn't as bad as it looks.

Pakistanis are one part drama queen and one part publicist—and are prone to near-hysterical exaggeration in both regards.

America and the West on balance aspire toward candor, forthrightness and modesty in their communications, in relative terms. Americans' crap detectors are set for a lower threshold. Pakistanis tend toward a style that could be perceived in the West as posturing, blustery and lacking in nuance.

Consider some unedited examples below from PakistaniLeaders.com, beginning with the page for Ansar Abbasi himself:

> Being a popular name in journalism today, he has a lot to do with the tomorrow of print media of Pakistan as well; and to talk of the past, Ansar has really established himself as an accredited name. So, he has covered a tough past, has shined out as a glittering star in the present, and holds a promising future waiting for him. Few are blessed with the kind of success Ansar has been blessed with.

With those kinds of credentials, I suppose I'd run around telling people I hate them too.

Take too the site's listing for Sadruddin Hashwani, a billionaire who built a hotel empire in Pakistan, which concludes thusly:

> Mr. Sadruddin Hashwani is a man of integrity whose ideas are worth admiring and his practices are worth emulating. His success story gives the nation a zillion lessons to learn. Mr. Sadruddin Hashwani, Hats off to you and thanks again. He is a true son of the soil, indeed !!!

Indeed. As you begin to see, posturing and exaggeration are all part of the theater of being Pakistani. Consider the case of Pakistani President Zardari, a man who just a few years ago argued he was mentally unfit to stand trial for corruption in England. His PakistanLeaders.com page spins the matter like this:

> Having spent a great deal of time in jails and detention on account of politically motivated trials, Asif Zardari has probably gathered what it takes to be a resilient political worker. Currently, assisting his son 'Bilawal Bhutto Zardari' to help manage the affairs of Pakistan Peoples' Party, he is indeed a major political figure today.
>
> Repeated arrests and detentions have made him a controversial political figure. However, his spirits are high and in spite of his deteriorated health owing to the agonies of imprisonment, he is agile and active and committed to the cause of democracy. …He has wide-ranging interests and loves horses among the animals.

The term "probably" is an unusual qualifier in the second sentence of the passage above, showing rare hedging and modesty. But for the most part there is little subtlety in Pakistan. Look at the country's ostentatiously decorated buses and trucks and homes and clothing and jewelry, and you will encounter a riot of colors and shimmers and sparkles. Their food is not mild: their savories are howlingly spicy, their indigenous desserts are shockingly sweet. When they paint, they paint in the most vivid tones, and so it is when they speak: Within interpersonal communication, tongues are hammers and words are nails, and each sentence is an expression of cosmic stakes.

As you'd expect, Pakistanis who have grown up in the West tend to be so different in their style of communication and even thought, that they often are at wit's end in dealing with kinfolk, bureaucrats and media from the motherland. My own relationship with my father, a proud, naturalized American who came here 53 years ago, often captured this.

After 9/11, if my friends would mention to Dad their concern that Pakistan harbored many who would seek to destroy the West, he always comforted them by stressing that "a very, very tiny number of people—maybe .001% of the population—supports these extremists."

Later, in a private moment, he would fret about how fellow Pakistanis weren't giving enough financial support to a school he founded in his hometown village to offer an anti-extremist education to local children. "How can we keep Pakistan from being destroyed by the extremists if we don't offer children good schools?" he would ask darkly.

"But you said we only had .001% crazy people over there, so it can't be that bad, right?" I'd ask in return. Sarcasm never did translate well across cultures within our house. Recall too that my defying my father's instruction in life resulted in a bit of Drama Queen Theater, when he derided me as "the second-worst man alive"—behind Salman Rushdie.

Other family members would hasten to add that his words were an expression of passion rather than dislike: A betrayed father or mother or lover or friend speaks in angrier terms than does a detached observer—especially in Pakistan.

That gets back to the difficult matters facing Washington as it attempts to extend the steady hand of fellowship while dodging verbal bullets. They will have to bear in mind that Pakistanis' recent expressions of disgust toward the U.S. are real but also paper-thin. Those feelings represent a sense of betrayal that will not disappear overnight, but which is not necessarily permanent.

But Pakistanis also have their own challenge in moving from public drama to public diplomacy. Too much angry posturing by Pakistanis may not have the intended effect. Jimmy Carter came to office with irenic goals and ideals, and became a "born-again Cold Warrior" by the end of his term, as some experts described his reaction to over-steps by the Soviets.

The old joke goes: What do you call a Democrat who's been mugged? A Republican.

Pakistan's verbal muggers may need encouragement from their fellow citizens to tone it down, as American officials offer to help pull Pakistanis out of a hole that most will admit (in their more candid moments) is their own doing.

Arabs and South Asians would do well to stop "stomping on the ground"

A Reuters picture in the spring of 2003 was revealing. A grieved Jordanian man, dressed in traditional Arab garb, turned away from a television screen to hide his face in his hands. The source of his distress was the image on the screen above him: An American GI placing a U.S. flag over the face of a statue of Saddam Hussein.

Visiting Ferhan a few weeks later, I listened to his concerns about how that televised image of the flag would smolder in the minds of Arabs and South Asians, who would resent the implied notion of an occupation. Looks like he called it correctly.

Yet that same weekend his first daughter Emaan provided a political parable. Now 18 months old, she was more dangerously energetic and active than ever. She had a tendency to jump up and down on chairs, fall and bonk her head on the floor, and howl bloody murder.

Once Emaan kicked into banshee mode, she wouldn't pull out of that mode with gentle words or a hug or a kiss on the boo-boo. She needed you to beat the ground. Stomp on it angrily. And maybe kick the chair too. Once you'd punished the floor thusly and warned it to never hurt her again, she settled down a bit. "Go," she then snapped tearfully at the chair, gesturing for it to leave her life.

Do adults act like infants? Far too often. So do entire citizenries. Few citizenries have bonked their heads in the past half-century as often or as visibly as Saudis, Palestinians and Pakistanis, and few have been guiltier of perpetuating their own nightmares.

And yet too many constituencies on "the street" have passed judgment: The ground must be beaten. Someone kick something. Anything. We're tired of always being the one who gets publicly humiliated.

Cynical and repressive Arab governments have encouraged this projection of rage and guilt in every external direction. Should these societies reform themselves internally, it would result in these dynasties losing power and privilege.

While American foreign policy has been simplistic and one-sided, the Arab street's response has been puerile and toxic. It will take some bold people in those nations to say, "Enough. Stop beating the ground and start learning how to walk like an adult." That talk can't come easily from the outside though. An Arab-American or Pakistani-American will get dismissed as an Uncle Tom for making such a case publicly. I speak from experience.

II. Lessons from the Bickering Gods

A little psychology and a little Sufism can produce Islam 2.0

Remember the Lord so vividly that you forget yourself.
Let the one who calls and the one who is called blend together,
lost in the Great Call itself.
—Jalaluddin Rumi, 13th century Sufi mystic

Come now, whoever ye may be,
You who wonder, you who seek to worship, it matters not who you be.
Ours is not a gathering of fear or despair.
Come alongside us, even if you have failed a thousand times
Still come, come alongside us.

—Rumi

During my years as an evangelical who was constantly reading theological writings for assurance that what I believed was true, I would come across Christian apologetics' examinations of Islam, which often showed that the Sufi, or mystical, branch of Islam had many similarities with Christianity. As noted by my friend Varun Soni, USC's dean of religious life, mystical traditions of most religions have a great deal in common. They tend to see a magnificent blurring of the boundaries between Creator and Created, and within Creation itself. That tends to make them all-embracing, tolerant, respectful and good-humored.

Reading Sufi passages, I often suspected that I could easily imagine myself as a Sufi and wondered if that would have made my parents happier, or if that would have kept jihadist militants from wanting to kill an apostate such as myself.

Hard to say. Good-natured, pluralistic Sufi mysticism undergirded the Islamic religion and cultural expression of the Indian subcontinent for centuries, but it's been displaced by a grimmer, Arabic Islam that sees Sufism as soft, and a bit heretical.

But if ever a great world religion needed a 2.0 update, Islam is it, and Sufism could be a major component.

Two days prior to this writing, I watched a Pakistani Dawn Television broadcast via satellite television in Orange County. It was the holy month of Ramadan, where good Muslims fast from sunrise to sundown. I sipped coffee as I watched a Western-dressed mullah discuss the proper manner in which a Muslim should give his obligatory charity (an annual tax of 2.5% of all possessions, called the *zakat*).

"One must remember that the condition of the heart is what matters most," he said. "The Sufis note that one must make a *zakat*, or sacrifice, of not just one's money, but one's heart, one's patience, one's commitment to serving others."

That's the crucial balance, in every great religion, between the state of the internal heart and the external actions of one's hands. And that balance is difficult: Jesus' great reforming work consisted of reminding pious, conservative Jews that their fasting and charity amounted to nothing if they were just done for external show, without the proper spirit. And yet the Christians who followed him managed to ignore such advice as they concocted theological formulas for salvation and killed one another over minor deviances from the theologically correct standards of the moment.

Islam has generally been a rules-oriented religion. But its Sufis, like Jesus and the apostle Paul, remind us that the letter of the law matters less than the spirit. That's why some of them can rationalize a gin and tonic, that's why they don't sweat every last edict. Like Augustine, they believe that a person should "Love God, and do as you please."

Augustine didn't mean that you should constantly be drunk and incontinent. He meant that if you genuinely love and enjoy God, you'll do the right thing by and by, without nervously sweating the details in the manner that so many Southern Baptists, Catholics and Muslims do.

The Sufis get that. And if more Muslims begin to get that again, Islam will mellow and adapt in ways that benefit its adherents and others.

But Sufis will have to take some lumps first, because of the stern Mullahs who belittle it.

• • • • • • •

I suspect that Islam will increasingly be informed by Westernized Muslims delving into contemporary theories of psychology, which can help demonstrate where certain religious edicts reflect healthy boundaries and where they reflect mere hang-ups and cultural foibles. As a wise Sufi woman once told me, "Many of the rules that distinguish one religion from another are just examples of obsessive-compulsive behavior."

Now that's an intriguing concept: Think of the obsessive hand-washers who work in your office. Notice that they seem to get sick more often than everyone else anyway. Think of religious ritual hand-washing within religion. A wise person will find themselves wrestling with whether to worry less about the letter of the law, with its exhausting rituals and restraints, and focus more on the often life-giving spirit of the law.

Moderates are lousy soldiers, so don't expect them to win holy wars or culture wars

Let me quote my favorite pundit: Me. "The United States needs to observe with caution the internal battles within Mideastern Islam, while nurturing its forces of moderation," I wrote in the Seattle Times in 2007. "But we do not need to act as though the Islamic world is united against us. The Islamic world is united against nothing."

I stand by *most* of that statement.

I meant that the "war by Islam on the West" was a stunt used by reactionary jihadist forces to gain support from an Arab and Pakistani street whose admiration and envy for America were now outweighed by irritation with U.S. foreign policy.

I sensed that Western analysts and commentator-hawks of the Mark

Steyn or Fox News or Ben Shapiro stripe had eagerly gobbled the jihadists' bait in order to make their own self-serving case as prophets warning that the West needs to be tougher to destroy the supposedly unified forces of Islam. This alarmed me because it risked creating a self-fulfilling prophecy — polarizing moderate Muslims into believing that the West indeed seeks to destroy them.

But I do wonder if I've been too hopeful that moderate Muslims will win the day against the extremists, even though I still maintain that moderates are the great majority within Islam.

The reason is that moderates are wussies by nature. Extremists of the right or the left or religion or secularism live for a good fight. Moderates avoid fights. That's what makes them so moderate. They quietly fume about the extremist jerks out there, but they've got jobs to keep and mouths to feed. In a fight between a moderate and a martyr, who are you really going to put your money on?

What we need, in American politics as well as in the Muslim world, are what I'd call "radical centrists." These sorts of persons have a martyr streak in them, but they don't have one-sided ideological delusions or a certain nastiness. Maybe they're the only types that can live out Jesus' command to take a hit without hitting back. Only these types can take the blows that result from a real battle without escalating matters.

That takes rare courage. But I have no doubt that this world will be better when those repulsed by extremists and opportunists, in any country, stand up and show some spine in the face of such country-wreckers.

Learn to be a disappointment

Laura Robinson, a longtime psychologist-friend from Hollywood Pres, once said that the goal of a good therapist is to increase a client's capacity to experience disappointment. I'll do her one better by saying one of the chief goals of a healthy human being is to increase his or her own capacity to be a disappointment.

I grew up torn between wanting to be a star and wishing I could blend in. Both are self-absorbed positions, but the former is proactive while the latter is a defensive posture, based on my calculation that I'll draw more ridicule if people know who I am than if I don't stand out.

As I grew older and bolder, I believed right through my mid-30s that I could learn to express myself in way that would win as much applause as I coveted. I gave lectures at Hollywood Presbyterian and wrote articles for the church newspaper that earned some acclaim and some criticism, and always believed it was just a matter of time before I learned how to dial up the acclaim and dial down the disdain. Sure, people told me that no one can speak his mind truthfully and hope to be loved across the board, a truth which I knew from how my own family couldn't stand me at times, but I believed I carried enough tact in my quiver to eventually get the adoration of a vast audience.

It was ironic, then, that as I spent years searching for appreciation within the Christian church and looking for ways to amplify it more broadly within American society, I would later walk away from church. I spent many evenings lamenting all those lost Saturdays brushing up on Calvinist theology in the Fuller Seminary library.

As for my shocked church friends and mentors, many did their best to help me see how I was missing the point. I was a disappointment to them, as I'd earlier been a disappointment to my own family.

But I'd come to realize that the ability to be a disappointment to others is the key step to becoming the person you truly want to be.

And ultimately, the right people will no longer find you to be such a disappointment.

"True Believers" can dish it out but typically can't take it

When I speak of True Believers, I'm talking about anyone who believes in something and expects everyone else to believe it. Here I'm talking about conservative Muslims, evangelical Christians, hardcore atheists, militant feminists, in-your-face gay activists and so on.

I believe everyone could do well to read Eric Hoffer's incredible examination of True Believers, titled, appropriately, *The True Believer*. Not long after the last smoldering embers of World War II cooled, he looked at the whole herd of True Believers and offered wise insights into the insecurities and doubts and shared hatreds that often bound groups of believers together and coalesced them into mass movements.

Here are three observations of my own, based on my own best efforts to be a True Believer at various points:

When I am a True Believer:

1. I believe I am right, and others are wrong, and that it's not being judgmental for me to simply acknowledge that I have assented to God's truth whereas they have not assented;
2. I believe others are terribly judgmental for criticizing and disrespecting what I believe. For instance, "How can those secularists smugly think they're so much better than a man of faith such as me, when they're every bit as dogmatic....?"
3. I tend to forget that I need to be able to take whatever I feel called by my god to dish out. I want to be seen as unequivocally right; but if I am losing a debate, I will revert to requesting the basic courtesy and respect that all viewpoints deserve, even the dumb ones that I failed to defeat.

That's why many Muslims in America, outnumbered as they are, stand up for tolerance and pluralism in America, but haven't shed enough tears about the abuse of religious minorities within their own nations. And that's why evangelical Christians demand prayer and creationism in their schools but would want religion completely off the table if their kids were to be exposed to those other dangerous traditions.

It's more blessed to learn than to teach

As an evangelical for 15 years, I spent a great deal of time arguing alongside various theological friends and mentors that our faith was alive, dynamic and specific. We derided those people who mixed and matched spiritual traditions. We laughed about those misguided saps who identified themselves as "spiritual but not religious." We believed that only we, who looked upon Jesus with a particular view, had "passed from death to life," to use Jesus' own term.

Eventually I was able to admit that many of the most alive people I knew were "spiritual but not religious" persons, or Buddhists or new-agers. Some were not even spiritual. Yet they move from event to event with an intuitive sense of purpose, spontaneity and freedom, and bounced back easily from setbacks, neither rationalizing nor overanalyzing Providence's purposes for them. Many of the least alive people I knew were the "frozen chosen," grim guardians of Christian mores, neurotic people unwilling to dive into life.

• • • • • • • •

When I left evangelicalism behind, I didn't feel I'd changed as a person, but I felt as though I'd shed a straitjacket.

My attitude is that I'm happy for you if you're a person of faith who is happy in your faith. I applaud you if you feel that faithfully belonging to X or Y religion allows you to feel a greater connection with the human community and to make a greater contribution to our earth than if you were a Taoist or Hindu or a secular humanist or an empiricist who sees the interconnectedness of our cosmos.

If you are such a person, I don't shun you and I would hope you wouldn't shun me.

However, I just felt wearied of being so closely associated with another type of person, the type of person that I myself had been: One who feels his or her faith has little meaning unless it involves the great triumph of his own theology over all pretenders.

The evangelical approach no longer functions for me, not in terms of an ability to explain life experiences, predict life experiences, or alter life experiences. My decision to shed my evangelical skin was less of a sudden shift in perspective than an inevitable culmination tracing back years.

The spiritual journey, insofar as it joins all of us together, requires a decision about where to live with certainty and where to live in mystery. For evangelicals, certainty is simply too certain, mystery simply too absent.

Evangelicalism—or True Believerism of any stripe—reduces opportunities to grow and to learn due to its narrow boundaries. You may disagree, but you cannot say that your approach works for everyone—and saying that "my approach works for everyone and is the *only* thing that works for everyone" is pretty much the whole point of evangelicalism.

My evangelical years finally convinced me that, while a bunch of people claimed to have been renewed by the Holy Spirit, the processes of change that I once saw as supernatural were merely natural, relating to how the human mind works. A good psychologist accomplished more than a good pastor. A good antidepressant outperformed the Holy Spirit on most days.

One of the best aspects of the gospel, as it occurs to me, is that we can receive wonderful things from unexpected and even unwanted sources if we will just humble ourselves. This is implicit in the call to accept divine forgiveness and assistance rather than attempt to stand weakly on our own.

Given this, our pluralistic society would seem to afford evangelicals untold opportunities to find treasure within others' traditions and help them understand how God has made all of us rich.

But if a proper evangelical were to hear a wise word from a Hindu or Sufi or Buddhist, he would immediately attempt to prove that the speaker is wrong and in desperate need of evangelical wisdom.

Evangelicalism is inherently a fault-finding approach to spirituality: Everyone else is wrong, only we are right.

Yes, I know, it's ironic that I will accuse evangelicalism of this given how I am doing a good deal of fault-finding in this book. The distinction is that if evangelicalism or any other "exclusive" path is to be seen as worth the effort, it must live up to its lofty claims.

Hinduism and Buddhism do not make such exclusivity claims and thus do not need to be measured accordingly. Evangelicalism, however, asks for rigid allegiance and the forsaking of all other sources of wisdom. This reaches its zenith in the approach of Christian charismatics, who sniff out demons under every bed and in every closet.

It's one thing to believe, as evangelicals do, that the great Christian writer Phillip Yancey and Mother Teresa and those televangelist nuts Jan and Paul Crouch are powerfully connected and united in "the body of Christ." It's not plausible to me though, to believe that Phillip Yancey and Mother Teresa and the Dalai Lama and Gandhi have less of a connection. No, that seems wrong-headed and quite implausible. It is not true and not edifying to believe this. Rather, this takes what is enlightened in Christianity and turns it into naked tribalism.

I would choose to be richer than this, more willing to learn from others than simply to act as though they have little or nothing to teach me.

When I argued points such as these in an online discussion a few years back, I received the following response from one reader:

> If you followed Christianity because of Evangelicalism, you missed the point.
>
> It's about a relationship with the Father, who died for us... think about it, you are looking at an institution, not the Person. He hasn't failed you, nor will He ever. And yet, He will not share His glory with a Buddha or a Lama, or any other god. Return to your first love, Bro!

Sorry, "bro," I'm not coming back to your religious chauvinism. This reader needed above all to reinforce the exclusive correctness of his faith, otherwise such faith would apparently have no great value to him. That's why he needed to miss the point of pretty much all I had written. There's nothing for him to learn from the rest of the world, only things to lecture people about. In the end, it says much about how he handles his own doubts—by doubling down on his commitment to his one true path.

I instead preferred to get out there and try things that my evangelical friends and mentors would have found scandalous: new-age workshops on "spirit dancing" and tantra. For an in-your-head, over-analytical person such as myself, these get-into-your-body types of exercises were wonderful ways to grow. The odd rhythms and rituals would have sent a conservative Christian fleeing, denouncing them as demonic. But I found a certain catharsis in them. Hopping around like an ass wasn't for me for the long haul, but it was liberating as an occasional stretch of the body and spirit.

After you fall out of love with Jesus, you can still be friends

The whole notion that faith in Jesus made us a unique, heavenly community seemed too good to be true at some level. Yet it was great fun for a while, despite the headaches involved.

When you looked up at the skies, you believed that they were created with you in mind, and you knew that the infinite force behind them had your best interests in mind, even when you or others didn't have your true interests in mind.

Life wasn't to be seen as some grim test of your actions and your thoughts; it was a gracious invitation to be a part of a life-affirming community, part of a people who affirmed life so powerfully that it took on the qualities of eternity. It was a uniquely reconciling community that, in fits and spurts and flashes, gave you bright glimpses of heaven.

You just knew that the force behind all things seen and unseen was gracious and forgiving, because It, or He, preached loving one's enemies above fighting holy wars, called for praying for enemies rather than calling for revolutions, called for making peace through weakness, not through strength.

It, or He, did what you couldn't do in terms of paying for your mistakes, and in initiating a cycle of reconciliation throughout the cosmos. It, or He, swallowed up the pain of life and the burden of death, and showed us that the path to eternity involved our willingness to do the same.

It was dangerous and confusing and wonderful, this belief that the creator of the cosmos loved us so infinitely that it incarnated as one of us, and that we somehow shared in the content and character of this divine being. It was so dangerous and confusing that faithful people for 20 centuries banned and bullied and bludgeoned one another for getting even one of the accompanying trinitarian theological nuances wrong.

And yet it *was* wonderful: We were no mere monkeys, no mere random accidents, we were made in the image of this very creator, and we had a great mission to bring peace and goodness to our world, in a way that no religion or philosophy or government or army or non-profit organization could bring them.

This was "faith in Jesus," as I understood it. As a Pakistani-American who grew up in a Muslim environment, it seemed even more dangerous and confusing and wonderful.

The weekend church retreats were enjoyable and meaningful, as were the efforts to see every bum who walked in through the door as someone made in the image of God, someone who was in Mother Teresa eyes' nothing less than Christ himself in disguise. Even the church politics were enjoyable, as bold efforts to prod ourselves as fallen humans to prayerfully move to a better place; even the theological disputes were breathtaking efforts to put words on cosmic-sized mysteries.

This faith in Jesus was wonderful, but it also became quite exhausting, especially given the demand that it be seen and preached as unique.

Affirming that it was the sole, unique avenue to the reconciliation of humankind somehow had kept me in a state of tension with my own family for 15 years, and with many of my dearest friends and colleagues. Affirming its uniqueness meant I had to either convince others of their wrongness or quietly dismiss their eternal prospects. Affirming its uniqueness meant I had a lot to tell other people and not as much to learn.

Ultimately personal and global events conspired to make me fall out of love with Jesus, after 15 breathtaking years. Why? It had something to do with my realization that human beings are wired to fight. Wired maybe by Jehovah or Allah or Mother Nature or Brahma or by Natural Selection, but wired nonetheless to band into one group to fight another.

As far as I could tell, religion had as much of a shot at sanctifying the fighting impulse as it did of softening it. Certainly religion can be helpful or even necessary to the human condition. But I wasn't about to claim any longer that one was unique.

The post-9/11 revelation to me was that my religious faction seemed to have been assigned a more pacifistic blueprint and philosophy than the other ones—and yet ultimately those who belonged to it were just as able as anyone else to rationalize carpet-bombing.

The conservative bullies were good at rationalizing "a clash of civilizations," whether in Peoria or in Peshawar—but even the liberal academic pacifists seemed adept at, ironically, destroying the careers and reputations those who didn't acknowledge their zeitgeist of tolerance.

On the website of the famously contentious atheist/scientist Richard Dawkins, I found an intriguing comment by an atheist reader:

> I've been around enough Christian communities to know that Christianity is closer to being all things to all people than it is to being a clear unifying message to all. This perhaps is to me the most intuitively obvious flaw in the Christian theory of the universe.

That sums up why I walked away. Once I came to that sort of view, there was no reason to fight my family or a large segment of the world by continuing to affiliate so publicly with an exclusivist, evangelical approach that so antagonized others' sensibilities. Even if I didn't share their sensibilities, it was no longer a battle that was worth any amount of trouble on my part.

Some Christian friends told me I could still go to church just for the companionship and support even if I didn't believe the same things anymore about Jesus. That made sense: It was only when I left that I found out how many people lined church pews without inhaling Christian theology—they were just looking for friends or dates.

So sure, I reserve the right to go to whatever religious or nonreligious community I want in the future, while maintaining my intellectual independence this time.

And I'll tip my hat to some of the wonderful ideals of Jesus—right along with those of Prophet Muhammad, and of Moses and Buddha and Ramakrishna and Albert Einstein. Maybe we can all be friends. But we have a tough task ahead in teaching the zealots and the rabble-rousers and opportunists and jealous gods on all sides that their best interests lie more in a shared freedom of worship than in attempts to win battles of religious conversion.

The gods might give you a sign, but they hate you for asking

The apologetics and arguments came as a flood once I left church, as old Christian friends tried to convince me that I was merely frustrated with humans' inability to live up to the standards of Jesus, not with the power or goodness of Jesus himself. I could predict the arguments, because I'd used them myself for 15 years

I was told by church friends that, in walking away from Jesus, I had been confusing the institutionalized religion of Christianity with the greater, personal relationship with Jesus. I'd used lines like that once too, in discussing those who'd "fallen away from the truth." So now it was my time to shut up and take it.

There's a peculiar tension in Christianity: Jesus offers a miraculous sign in one town, then in the next town tells people they're idiots for wanting a sign. Christians believe prayer to Jesus has unrivaled power, but they also prepare you for the idea that most of the time God will answer your prayers with a gentle "nope."

All of that could have been acceptable if I could have managed to continue believing that it was indeed unique.

William Lobdell was an evangelical who zealously sought the religion beat at the *Los Angeles Times,* hoping to make sense of his Christian faith to a mass audience. As he saw Christianity up close as an investigative journalist, he ended up leaving his faith and the religion beat. In a memorable 2007 essay, he explained his actions:

> I understood that I was witnessing the failure of humans, not God. But in a way, that was the point. I didn't see these institutions drenched in God's spirit. Shouldn't religious organizations, if they were God-inspired and -driven, reflect higher standards than government, corporations and other groups in society?

That's the dilemma of the church. It's usually explained away by a "yes, but things don't always look different on the outside" response.

I had helped my old friend Tod Bolsinger with a book that was a response to the challenge of writer Martin Lloyd-Jones: If Christianity is what it seems to be, then Christians should be living exceptional lives.

Tod and I kept seeing that Christians were remarkably like everyone else—and I noticed they were more warlike than others because they saw global issues as battles of good versus evil. The irony is that I resolved the tension by deciding Christianity wasn't the sole, exclusive road to truth.

Tod resolved it by falling back on a peculiarly Christian belief that, although faith in Jesus is the only way to be regenerated by the Holy Spirit, Christians won't look any different from everybody else—until everybody else is shoved off into eternal damnation on the Last Day.

I suppose I had believed that myself at times in previous years, in the same effort to avoid chucking both the baby and bathwater of my Christian worldview.

Yet I also kept seeing that pagans and Hindus celebrated miracles of healing, agnostics showed gritty determination when faced with cancer, and my own Muslim father seemed far more willing to forgive slights and make peace than those to whom the gospel of reconciliation was entrusted.

Maybe that was the real sign from whatever gods may be up there: A sign that Christians have as much to learn from the rest of the world as they have to teach. But the evangelical approach to Christianity is too arrogant to ever place itself in the student's position.

Christian faith is built on a powerful notion of sin and redemption... that few believe in the clutch

My major home during my evangelical years, Hollywood Pres, was the home of Henrietta Mears, a dynamo single woman who made the church a magnet for college students—a neglected demographic to that point, since they seemed more transient than the young married couples that churches used as their financial and ministerial foundations. Henrietta's classes boasted hundreds of students from USC, UCLA and elsewhere, and she mentored scores of top evangelical leaders, including Billy Graham, Campus Crusade founder Bill Bright, future Bel Air Presbyterian founder Louis Evans Junior (the son of Hollywood Pres' famed senior pastor), future New Testament authority Dale Bruner and many others.

Hollywood Pres' influence in its heyday was a deep source of pride for its members at that privileged moment—and became a haunting legacy for the church in later years, when a new generation of leaders found it harder to mimic Henrietta's impact in a post-*Happy Days* era.

I told my politically conservative friends there that they were neglecting how their faith is defined by a shocking and controversial set of claims:

1. All of humanity is in a state of sin, a kind of living death.
2. Within this natural state, no one is good, not one, not even Gandhi or Buddha. All are as guilty as Hitler.
3. Individuals and institutions alike are flawed, which is why the PTA and the UN alike cannot be trusted to bring peace to a fallen world.
4. This sort of pervasive imperfection can only be addressed by cosmic atonement and by enlistment within a new kingdom that serves as an alternative to the kingdom of the fallen world.
5. This atonement and this new kingdom are marked by something that seems weak and foolish and dangerously naïve by worldly standards of common sense. But to those who believe, it is the power of God, and it is the only thing of eternal and infinite worth, silly as it may seem to those who are perishing within a fallen world.

The conundrum for 20 centuries of Christianity was that its adherents tend to subscribe both to these principles and to the principles of the culture in which they live—and when the principles are in conflict, the prevailing culture usually wins. Iraq seemed yet another in a long line of examples in which Christians themselves become the ringleaders for anti–New Testament thinking.

I told such friends they were correct in noting that governments have different duties than individuals within a church. But I argued that, in that case, they should have a detached, resigned view that "the state will choose to go to war once in a while and we must pay the taxes that finance this war," and they should then go about your business within the Church that is supposed to reflect Christ's Kingdom more than the state is intended to. They should be more mindful of how good intentions go awry in a fallen world. More aware of how much Jesus discussed the laws of unintended consequences as they relate to the use of power and force.

Jesus noted that "where your heart is, there too your treasure is," and flag-waving evangelicals' hearts and treasures seemed filled with yellow ribbons saluting the nation's war-making forces. Whereas Jesus pronounced a blessing on peacemakers, America had used the term for a nuclear missile; I hadn't before noticed how evangelicals had never seen an irony there.

It seemed as we marched into Baghdad in 2003 that no religious doctrine and no "act of regeneration by the Holy Spirit" was potent enough to overcome the natural tribalism placed within us by Mother Nature. Religious devotion sanctified latent hawkishness by providing a crusading framework for foreign policy—despite the New Testament notion that human depravity prevents any one nation from proclaiming itself to be morally superior to others.

Strive to judge world events with intellectual consistency, even though your emotions won't cooperate

If Islam, which is 1,400 years old, were a lesser religion than two-millennia-old Christianity, we face a difficult task in explaining how Christianity has witnessed similar problems on its watch even when it was a more advanced age.

Mainly I just credited Christianity for causing the Enlightenment and tried my best to dismiss the possibility that Enlightenment was a reaction against Christendom, coming as it did 17 centuries after the Church was born.

I ignored too charges that Christian soldiers in the Crusades represented a negative force. As I drifted from warlike American evangelicalism, I not surprisingly found myself staring in a new light at what I'd earlier skipped over or refused to investigate.

I'd known that Martin Luther was a jerk, but I spent more time considering the full scope of his teaching.

"Now just behold these miserable, blind, and senseless people," he wrote in 1543 in one of his lesser-known books, *On the Jews and Their Lies*. In a manner that would fuel generations of German anti-Semitism, Luther advised his countrymen to burn synagogues and raze Jewish homes, "in honor of our Lord and of Christendom."

Over in Geneva, under the influence of the brilliant theologian John Calvin, allegations of blasphemy and unbelief typically led to people being burned or hanged. Paintings and statues of religious figures—even reverential works—were as forbidden as any caricature of a Muslim prophet. Dancing was a jailable offense.

As former president George Bush would say, these pillars of Western civilization hated the freedoms that we enjoy.

So if some evangelicals can rationalize the lapses of Protestantism's greatest leaders in light of historical issues or the prevailing culture of that era, 16 centuries after Christ, they'd need to be equally charitable regarding Muslims' foibles today, 1,400 years into their own journey of faith.

U.S. evangelicals can view their religion as peaceful, despite believing in the absolute authority of a Bible whose God directed his people to take conquered women as plunder (a true family-values conundrum). In Deuteronomy 20, God also instructs his followers: "in the cities of the nations the Lord your God is giving you as an inheritance, do not leave alive anything that breathes." Yet the same evangelicals insist that relatively milder passages in the Quran are a sign of Islam's inferiority.

I'm not sure I score many points when I argue this publicly, though. I wrote a 2006 *Orange County Register* piece arguing the above, attempting to use my status as a Presbyterian elder to add some authority.

I got this note from a reader:

> The worst fears of any of us on this planet do not lie in our imaginations or our memories, but before our eyes on a daily basis, as long as you and your Muslim Brethren think it's acceptable to apply millennia old behaviors, like decapitating people with knives and shooting charity volunteers in the back and blowing up thousands of innocents in the name of your god, whenever you all are insulted. You are pathetic.

I also received this one:

> Yeah right....a pure traitor of his faith....defending Islam and bashing Christianity...Yeah right elder at an Evangelical Church! Pure Poser!

That was interesting. As mentioned earlier, way back in 1995, before the war on terror, a friend at Hollywood Pres confided that someone warned him that I may just be a Muslim wolf in the Christian henhouse.

Here's another email I received, addressed to me and the editor:

> In regard to Mr. Asghar's article, "Amazingly Graceless toward Islam" which appeared in the Paper on Thursday, Oct. 26. It was sad to see Islamist's Propaganda gracing your paper. The Pope, whom you dismiss as unworthy of praise does not fervently command his faithful to murder anyone who does not agree with you; Instead, the Pope preaches peace, forgiveness and compassion for victims of War and Disease. He speaks to the social and spiritual welfare of not just the Western Hemisphere but for the World. In the future why don't you stick to selling your op-ed trash to Al Jazeera. God Bless You.

Yeah, buddy, go tell my parents that I spew Islamist propaganda all day. In my writing career, I've been a moderate, but I've always noticed that whenever I tilt even slightly to one side within a particular debate, the person on the other side condemns me for being an extremist representing the other side. It's psychological projection converted into a cosmic struggle.

I'll admit that I got some positive responses to my *Register* piece too, but the negative feedback is what rattles around forever in our brains.

I couldn't resist temptation, and offered the following retort to the first guy:

> How very odd: You say that we decapitate people whenever we feel insulted, and then you insult me by calling me pathetic. In any event, thanks much for taking the time to write. God bless you!

And I got this response:

Which is why I'll remain anonymous and prevent you and your buddies from decapitating me. Why not learn a few lessons from the people you mocked in your ridiculous piece in the OCR and knock off the violence and join the human race—in this century?

Sigh. Outwitted by a nitwit. But it frustrated me that he couldn't see my point. I was decrying violence in this century and in every century, and pointing out that no religion or civilization is immune to it.

Christian theology is based on the idea that we are all "sinful" and "fallen" and "depraved," so Christians more than anyone should be guided by their religious leaders to understand the New Testament notion that no one is to judge others before judging oneself. But I found almost no evangelical leaders, including the ones I'd worked with closely, to be willing to make such an argument publicly. They were too busy trying to keep their churches together and providing for their families. I understood, but it still saddened me.

Life is ultimately about art, not about faith or fact

After I left the evangelical movement, I didn't move from faith to perfect faithlessness, though I certainly have my agnostic days. Rather, I came to believe that all life is poetry. Poetry is the art of interpreting cold facts with the warming fire of cosmic meaning; and all meaningful and powerful spirituality is poetry. The literalists hate poetry and hate paradox, and that is why they tend to turn the best of spirituality into chest-beating organizational demands.

I'd argue that the only person who has a good prayer life is a person with an overactive imagination. By that, I mean that the two are the same thing. And that that can be a good thing. Imagination seems to be what allows a person to see a block of wood and infuse it with miraculous powers and personality; or to see the heavens and imagine there a cosmic battle of powers and principalities; or to toss heavenward a thousand petitions, see three of them get answered, and chalk it up to divine intervention. That interpretive power is the power of a poet.

The more supple true believers speak eloquently of prayer as being less an enterprise to get results and more of a primal, powerful need for us to be in communion with the Living God; that this interaction shapes us. C.S. Lewis said while his wife was dying, "Prayer doesn't change God, prayer changes me" (at least Anthony Hopkins said so while portraying him in *Shadowlands*); Oswald Chambers said, approximately, that prayer does not change things as much as prayer changes me, then I change things." This I buy. Yet this is in fact a more liberal, more "reasonable," more poetic interpretation of reality, which flies in the face of evangelicalism's supposed fact-based approach.

Dancing and religion aren't that different, and you can miss the joy in either

During the swing dance craze of the late 1990s in L.A., all the girls I wanted to date could be found at the Derby, made famous by the movie *Swingers*. I went there and took as many classes as I could, but I always struggled with getting both the steps and the rhythm right.

One night, I swinged, or swung, with a woman who noticed that I wasn't holding up my end of the dance bargain. "Okay, something's not right," she said.

I said, "Well, I think I'm doing all the right steps, aren't I? Slow, slow, quick-step, slow, slow, rock-step?"

She said, "Yeah, I know. But it's… it's not dancing."

True. Going through the steps isn't dancing. I did love my chances to swing with Kate, who was bouncy and fun on the dance floor, and who could encourage me to have fun even if my technique wasn't perfect.

Here's the link between religion and dancing: Dancing involves a certain joyful movement that uses certain movements as a framework. Religion attempts to do the same. The great religions preach gratitude, happiness and humility, using a framework built on guidelines and commandments.

You can go through the motions of either dancing or religion in a joyless, dutiful fashion. It becomes a grim affair, the difference being that you don't believe you'll go to hell for dancing poorly (it will only feel like hell, especially if you're trying to impress a cute girl).

Ideally, you should be dancing with joy and passion, and your excellent footwork will reflect the quality of your dance. But most of us don't get both the joy and the footwork down. Most religious people focus on the footwork of their faith and not the joy.

On the dance floor and in life, I came to realize that I'll take an imperfect but joyful and passionate dance over excellent footwork that's not really dancing.

Gold's Gym and Thomas Aquinas don't have all the answers

"Yes there are two paths you can go by, but in the long run there's still time to change the road you're on." That's Robert Plant's cryptic line from *Stairway to Heaven*, which many evangelicals believed was a sly invitation to worship Satan. After all these years of listening to Led Zeppelin, while I may value Old Luke's counsel, I certainly don't worship the gent.

In any event, I don't believe that all roads lead to Heaven, or to salvation (whatever those may be) but it's hard for me to believe that one road works infallibly and that all other roads are lacking. But for some reason, we tend to like that notion, which creates incredible marketing opportunities for charlatans and salesmen in religion and in health and medicine and in business and in pretty much every area of life. Everyone's got a miracle cure that's the "only solution."

Some old Hollywood Pres friends speculated that I grew away in faith because I'm admittedly a compulsive person, either all in or all out.

One friend wondered if I got tired of church because I grew too intensely involved and needed a break. That implied that I'd be back once I get some rest. I shared how one friend had even mentioned a few years ago that I was like a guy who'd built up big spiritual muscles at the gym but needed a season of rest (and, I assume, a season of spiritual flab).

My response, staying with that metaphor, was that I had rather come to realize that there is more than one way to work out, more than one way to get healthy, more than one formula for being "in shape."

I was reminded of this when I went back to working out with a personal trainer at Gold's Gym. The trainer, Dmitri, had a strong point of view about what constitutes "being fit," at a cardio and muscle level. But it was a different view from that of past trainers. Confused, I consulted a friend who was an independent trainer, who said my new trainer had a typical "Gold's Gym mentality," which has a bias toward buffness rather than cardio fitness or leanness. So who in hell has the infallible formula? Who knows? But all trainers *believe* they have the right formula. All of them think they have the "one true path" to wholeness. They have *faith* that their way is right. And they want you and me to buy in, to the tune of thousands of dollars.

I am skeptical that any of them has a monopoly on the one true path of health. I sense I have different things to learn from a number of them, but that I must ultimately find for myself what is true for me. I'm not sure I believe that the Gold's way or the Bally's way or the 24 Hour's way reflects the truest way.

I can understand the need for people to commit to one way, rather than being all over the map each new week. But I still wonder if more variety would be good for them.

I believe we have to see religious views of salvation ("the path I follow is the one true path which all should follow") the way we see health regimens.

Every fitness instructor has her own theory of how to get truly healthy, and this usually involves comically contradictory dogmas and doctrines, just like what you see in religion.

Before Gold's, I had spent two years at 24 Hour Fitness in Long Beach, where the spin class instructors preached that you should never cycle with low resistance, as it's damaging to your knees. But the Gold's instructors now were hammering me to go ever faster with ever less resistance for extended stints. Some trainers have forced me to sprint up the steps in between weight training, to keep my heart rate high. Others warned that keeping my heart rate that high was withering my muscles.

Every expert has a different opinion that reflects her school of thought: Some preach stretching and flexibility, some don't; some love cardio, some don't.

My Gold's trainer told me that lemon water would reduce salt bloating, so I bought some lemons on the way home. The Internet had wonderful articles about how lemons will work weight miracles and make my skin shiny and new. But then other articles said that lemon water will also wash away more valuable minerals, including calcium. And yet... still other articles said lemon helps *retain* calcium. Others said it's pure acid.

What to do...?

I think the reason so many people are dogmatic about religion, or about their health approach, is precisely because it's so confusing, and so contradictory, and so many paths go in so many different directions. No, not all paths lead to Mt. Olympus—but no two people can seem to agree fully on how to even get near the damned mountain.

If a few of them realize they do agree, they form a tight community which invites others to share this "absolute truth" and which ridicules anyone who resists this so-called truth. Their zeal to expand their flock is directly proportional to their level of inner doubts about whether they're on the right path.

One kind of person will get cynical, lay on the couch with some Lay's, and get obese. Another one makes a decision on one way, then puts on blinders and shouts about how his way is the best way.

The best approach, I think, involves using some intellectual and moral independence in making those trade-offs and choosing a path without feeling an overpowering need to assert that "every knee shall squat and every ab shall crunch to the glory of my gym's way."

Miracle pills are nice, but most of us have to live life the old-fashioned way—through hard work

In the preceding section I squeezed to a pulp the notion that various salesmen of health regimens and religious doctrines posture as though they alone have the keys to the kingdom. Indeed our technological, attention-deficit era more than most may be addicted to the notion of miracle pills that allow us to circumvent the laws of physics and reality.

This stimulant will give you enough energy to keep you alert without sleeping a full eight hours. That pill will boost your thyroid activity enough that you can eat chocolate cake without gaining an ounce of fat—even if you never exercise. This quick visualization technique will give you peace and confidence without having to do the messy work of understanding and sorting out your inner turmoil.

Sure, maybe. Such claims aren't an outright lie. For a few people, such pills and techniques to accomplish miracles.

But all the best scientific evidence suggests that there is only one medication that is guaranteed to work for any ailment: And that's a placebo.

In fact, the miracle cures mentioned above may work for a few special people not because of their inherent properties, but because of the placebo effect.

That's why I can't ultimately scoff at any one person's faith in his god or his medicine—because if he really believes in it, it usually carries some value. That's the true "gift" of faith.

But not all of us can find the poetic faith in what our physical trainer or spiritual guru is telling us. Or we can find such faith, but only for a while. Then when we begin to doubt, we find we can never resuscitate the placebo's miraculous powers.

And for us, we have to go back to the basics, and do the hard work that seems to underpin life. It's not complicated, really: You and I know that a good body requires a sensible diet and an active lifestyle. We know that an all-fat, no-vegetables, couch-potato regimen isn't good for us, and we're dubious that any pill or philosophy could ever subvert this reality.

It's not that different in terms of religion or spirituality. The universal basics seem to indicate that altruism makes us happier than selfishness; that we are all connected and interdependent, and that hurting others hurts ourselves; that accepting reality on its own terms, and meditating on the nature of things, will keep us mentally balanced and poised; and so on.

But what happens all too often is that someone turns the universal basics into an exclusive truth—and that sets the stage for conflict. For example, Jesus' telling his followers that "anyone who loses his life for my sake will find it" could be seen as a sign of the universal truth that we only find our true selves by losing ourselves in a purpose bigger than ourselves, but orthodox believers have often turned it into an exclusive formula for salvation—one that has at times been used to justify intolerance.

I realize that many (or most) people crave the feeling that they are part of an exclusive group of stewards of cosmic truth—that's their placebo, in fact, which gives them more confidence than if they believed that they simply favored one cultural expression of higher truths.

But I believe the better way is to pass up that false certainty. Blessed is he who can live without such a placebo.

Most people can't tolerate mystery

After my conversion, Dad trumpeted the merits of Prophet Muhammad. "He's the greatest lawmaker ever. Many Westerners have agreed," he often liked to say.

"Yeah," I would respond, "but the Old Testament was filled with laws, and the Pharisees of Jesus' time held to those rules rigidly. Jesus told them they had to focus less on the legalisms and more on the condition of their heart. The Quran seems to roll the whole thing back to Old Testament days. You say that Islam embraces Jesus, but it doesn't seem to embrace any of the teachings that even atheists believe he offered. Maybe the Quran was God's way of introducing monotheism to Arabs, and I can respect that, but I don't feel it's for everyone."

The debates also continued with Mom.

"Robbie, why do you believe that Islam is less peaceful than Christianity? Doesn't the Old Testament have so many stories about wars? Isn't God very vengeful there?"

"Well, yeah, maybe. But the New Testament changed all that." This was a hard one for me. I had done my best to ignore the Old Testament, precisely because it seems so different from the manner in which Jesus operated. Later my Christian theological mentors would tell me that I was wrong, and that the New Testament didn't negate the Old Testament; I would go on to spend years rationalizing Old Testament violence with these mentors.

Mom, though, continued to pepper me with questions. "What do you find so offensive about our teachings, Robbie?"

"Well, I think the Islamic approach is big on specific rules and regulations. The Christian view is that God loves you and that you do good things for him in a natural and heartfelt way. The Muslim view is that you have to do good things in order to win his favor. The Muslim view is just focused on the externals, not on the condition of the heart."

"That's not true at all!" Mom protested. "You don't even understand Islam. We believe in the condition of the heart. We do things because of who God is and because we're grateful. The great Muslim leaders would teach that, when you eat an apple, you should marvel at how God created that apple. Then, even eating an apple becomes an act of worship."

I could say amen to that. Fundamentally, though, we disagreed on various issues about the nature of morality and forgiveness and grace. And we disagreed about the nature of Jesus.

"So tell me, Robbie, about Jesus," Dad would say. "What is wrong with the way we see him? We see him as a good and exalted prophet, right up there with Prophet Mohammed."

"Well, Muslims don't recognize any of his teachings, for one thing. But beyond that, if you see him just as some human prophet, you'll miss the point, which is that he showed us the true character of God, and that his death and resurrection give meaning to our lives."

"Fine. But why do you need to believe he is the Son of God? That's sinful to think that God would have a son. He does not need a son, and he would not have a child with a woman."

"I'm not saying he needs anything, Dad. And I'm not saying he had sex in order to have a child. To say he was God's son is a way of saying he was God incarnate. He was God in human form."

"What? If he came down in human form, then no one was above running the universe!"

"It's not like that. Both could happen."

"How?"

"It's hard to put into words. It's... a paradox. A mystery thing."

Mystery be damned. Dad believed faith should be simple and direct: One God to follow, who clearly delineates rules that order human and social conduct. I felt that something a lot more mysterious was at work, that showed who God truly is and who we are truly meant to be.

But I'll admit that many people in all religions tend to value mystery only when they get to the point that they can't rationalize a particular belief in their own head. Some get to the point of mystery before others.

• • • • • • •

Evangelical Christians embrace literalism whenever possible (more accurately, whenever it suits their purposes), and mock poetic, symbolic interpretations of the Bible as being too liberal—except in those cases when literalism simply won't hunt as well as liberalism (e.g., explaining how Judas died in two entirely different ways).

Yet the New Testament is very liberal, very poetic, very symbolic. Most evangelicals have taken poetry and made it a science, just as their more fundamentalist brethren have taken Genesis 1 and made it a creation science: God is immutable and Jesus is the same yesterday, today, forever—yet the logos took on a human soul 2,000 years ago and then ascended back to the Godhead with that human soul, which seems to indicate that God is not immutable, nor is the *Logos*.

If you're going to be religious, it seems the best resolution is to take a poetic, liberal view of the matter, or to go through mental gymnastics in order to find an answer that's implausible to outsiders but which lets you sleep through the night, secure that you're still a "follower of the only way."

Evangelicals still have an opportunity to make a contribution through their beliefs

After 9/11, American evangelical leaders had an incredible opportunity to bring some salt and light to their flocks and to their communities, their nation and their world.

They blew it.

The restless flocks coalesced around neoconservative worldviews that were less founded on the distinct message of the New Testament and more on classical notions of good crushing evil. And pastors and theologians—with the very visible exception of Greg Boyd—failed to correct their flocks about the true nature of the faith they professed.

Boyd to me was one of the few good guys. He was pastor of an evangelical megachurch in St. Paul, Minnesota. Alarmed by the conflation of Christianity and conservative politics, he began to draw a line publicly in his sermons during the 2004 election. He argued that the sword (the government) and the cross (the church) shouldn't be seen as one unit. The New Testament respected the government's prerogative to run society, but the church was never meant to exalt a human institution such as government.

It was classic Pauline theology. But his truth-telling resulted in 1,000 members leaving the church. True, 4,000 members stayed behind—but any organization that suddenly loses 20% of its membership is going to struggle.

Boyd stayed bold. He wrote a powerful book, *The Myth of a Christian Nation*, in which he elaborated on several core New Testament themes. He used Biblical scholarship to denounce notions that America, or any state, was privileged in the eyes of God. He noted that the Christian church's imperative regarding enemies is to bless them and pray for them, not to bomb them—which is precisely why he said that Christians must stay out of the government's affairs of the sword.

Boyd preached the basics: Jesus said that blessedness didn't come from punching enemies but from bearing their pain; Paul said that security didn't come through wars or through citizenship in powerful empires, but through faith in Christ. If Christians believed this, the wake of 9/11 was one of the most powerful moments to live this out.

If there were a thousand Greg Boyds active within American evangelicalism, the world would be a different place. But there are precious few of them so far. Most preachers and theologians are too timid to challenge their congregations, even if they privately agree that Boyd's assessment reflects the best Christian theology. Many preachers typically say they are called to "be pastors to their congregations, not prophets." But Boyd was both pastor and prophet, and a powerful voice emerged that articulated the best within the evangelical tradition. I hope it doesn't remain a lone voice.

III. Lessons from the Clash of Cultures

What racism? It's better not even to notice other's hostility
I mentioned earlier that Seneca once argued that, if you think someone has slighted you but aren't sure, just move on and believe that he didn't. You'll be far better off for it.

In that sense, I was proud that Dad didn't complain about racism that was around him in North Carolina in the 1950s, and that he did not resign himself to a life with limits.

Although he knew his status as a Pakistani led people to come up with real or imaginary rules against hiring him, he focused on the fact that most people seemed to treat him just fine. This was a man with no chip on his shoulder. He kept moving forward, hoping it would work out, and that allowed him to get to a better place.

I do believe today that injustices are real and harsh; and yet those who stop to complain about them are the ones who often end up sinking in the quicksand of destiny. Dad wouldn't do that.

Ironically today, too many Pakistanis, and Muslims as a whole, are prone to just that sense of victimization. And even American conservatives have ironically become chiefs among whiners. As the *Economist* noted in the 2008 campaign:

> Conservatives make a good case that treating minority groups as victims diminishes America and institutionalises dependency. But when it comes to election-time they not only play the politics of victimhood,

but play it with extraordinary relish, presenting ordinary Americans as the victims of diabolical conspiracies.

Clashes of civilizations are sometimes just sibling rivalries, taken too far

Allow me to add a little context for our family's move from a once-proud Muslim empire to the now-proud West. Let's go, oh, all the way back to 2300 BC, to give it the proper religious context. That's when Abraham was said to have heard a call from the living God.

He and his son, Isaac, and their descendants, Jacob and Jacob, would be the patriarchs of Israel. Abraham's other son, Ishmael, would be sent away, but would become the patriarch of the Arab peoples, who would become the patriarchs of a worldwide Islamic faith.

Jesus arrived on the scene in 0 A.D., or more likely a few years earlier. Christians and Muslims alike believe he was born of a virgin through an act of the Spirit of God, that he performed miracles and that he will return at the end times, but the agreement ends right about there. Muslims are horrified by the thought that Jesus was crucified and resurrected, that he had a divine nature, or that he could claim any manner of equivalence with God. They often are especially offended by the insinuation that God would incarnate and thus need to do a Number 1 or Number 2.

Muhammad found his calling as a prophet in the Arab city of Mecca, six centuries after Jesus' ministry. And after a few more centuries, his followers rolled into the Indus Valley, the land of Dad's ancestors. They claim they won converts through their piety, while devout Christians and Hindus claim they used the sword to spread their faith. Muslims respond that Christians used the sword to spread their own faith, and that someone needed to save the Indus region from a terrible caste system and traditions such as the immolation of widows. And so it goes, with each side taking the brightest view of its own spiritual ancestry and the dimmest view of its opponents.

Islam long dominated regions of southern Europe and served as the world's most advanced civilization in terms of science and culture. The

Indus Valley produced chess and the number zero, and Islam spread and advanced such developments.

The various children of Abraham mixed together tensely during Islam's first millennium. Whether you believe that the Church's sins during the Crusades were regrettable or overblown, Muslims were far more embracing of Abraham's original Jewish tribe, as a trip to Israel's Museum of David would attest. Crusaders found it easier to massacre Jews than to live with them. (Now many evangelical Christians like to catch alienated Muslims quoting anti-Semitic literature that was written in the West as evidence that Islam is cruel).

Christian Europeans pushed Islamic regimes back around the 1600s; Arab culture soon stagnated and was horrified to see pale-skinned, non-bathing European "barbarians" pass it by. The rise of the West's Old World led to the unimaginable rise of the West's New World. America emerged as the pinnacle of human achievement. Islam and the West, both children of Abraham in a spiritual sense, would again cross paths. But this time the West held the position of power and prestige.

It was in this sort of context in which we came to America and in which I came to wish I could be a true American.

• • • • • • •

Mom came to spend a few days with me and my atheist roommate Jeff in 1990, and Jeff later chuckled while recounting to me her probing interrogation.

"Are you very interested in religious things, Jeff?" she asked.

"No, ma'am, not really."

"How about most of your friends? Do they worry a lot about religion?"

"Uh…. I'd have to say no."

"Hmm. Then what's the matter with Robbie?"

Hearing him tell me the story, I laughed too. But then I felt peeved. Jeff spent his time getting drunk and futilely attempting to get laid by someone he would hopefully never meet again. I was going to church, praying, giving to charity, and spreading peanut butter on crackers for

Sunday School kids even though I hate the smell of peanut butter. Yet Mom thought I was the oddball. (Looking back at it, I suppose I was).

You would expect Muslims and Christians to be united in their dislike for shallow, worldly lifestyles (which Jeff did grow out of in time). But their own sibling rivalry makes that impossible. They can be less threatened by debauchery or by atheism than by closely related religions—which to me is a tragedy that reveals human nature.

This doesn't just happen between distinct religious faiths. When you see how appalled a Catholic mother can be to see her child become a Protestant, you realize it happens within faiths. Indeed, the bloody religious wars of Europe and the Sunni-Shia battles within Islam, along with even the ridiculously overblown culture wars within the U.S., show how easy it is to fight over the silliest of nuances.

That's human nature, and reminds me of an old joke:

A pastor is just checking into his room in a 25-story downtown hotel, when a hotel employee begs him to come and talk a man off the ledge of the top story.

The pastor agrees, and begins to talk warmly to the despondent man on the ledge. "You have a lot to live for, son. Don't you believe in a good, loving God?"

"I do," said the man.

"Great," said the pastor. "And are you a Christian? Do you believe that Jesus takes away all your sins and pain?"

"Yes. I do. I'm a Presbyterian."

"Terrific! So am I! Are you a member of the Presbyterian Church of America, or the Presbyterian Church of the USA?"

"I'm with the PC-USA," the man replies.

"Heretic," the pastor says, as he shoves the man off the ledge.

Immigrants should embrace their names, which can provide hours of amusement to others

Relocating always results, for an immigrant child, in an opportunity for a new set of teachers to bungle your name.

For years, my family spelled my proper name as *Saqib Suhrab Asghar*.

Peers already had been having a field day with that, if not an outright Olympics.

My parents decided to do me a favor when I was small and Americanized my name, turning *Suhrab* into *Robbie*. However, they didn't Americanize it as much as they could have, spelling it *Rabi*. How many amusing ways can you come up with to pronounce that name? Ten-year olds find a few. Even well meaning schoolteachers warped it unintentionally.

By the time I was 12, Shabi offered me brotherly advice: "Look, just change the spelling of your name. Start writing *Robbie* on all your papers, so that it looks like what it's supposed to sound like."

That was some of the best advice I had gotten from him. I did so. This outraged one blond, all-American friend named Dave. "Dude," he protested, tossing back his golden locks, "you're turning your back on your heritage."

"Turning my back on what? It's just a nickname. It's an Americanized nickname. I should be able to spell it in an Americanized way. I should be able to spell it however I want."

"Well, I think you're turning your back on your heritage."

"Whatever."

Moving to Southern California in 1980 brought a new turn of events as it related to my sense of identity. Mom and I stood in the offices of Newbury Park High School, where I was registering as a sophomore. As she filled out a parental form, she told me, "Robbie, do you know what? I looked at your birth certificate, and it turns out we have been spelling your name wrong all these years."

"Hmm?"

"Your real name. It's not really *S-A-Q-I-B*. There's a U in it."

"What? Where?"

"It's *s-a-q-U-i-b*. It's a silent *u*. It sounds the same, but it has a *u*. We'll just put it on all your papers the right way from now on."

"Oh, geez, mom, don't do that! *Saquib*? Everyone's going to mispronounce it! They'll call me *Sah-kwib* or something."

"But it's your real name."

"Mom, we've made it this far. Let's not mess with tradition."

"No, we will just go with the proper spelling."

"Aw.... nuts."

I seemed to get through that next year without much trauma, as most teachers just asked me to pronounce my strange name, at which point I asked them to just call me *Robbie*. I did have the usual butterflies that accompanied being the new kid in school, and showing up in October to boot, so that you stand out even more as the strange newcomer.

But the next year, eleventh grade, was less smooth. My first period class was taught by Mr. Crouch, a large, burly man who loved to tease the nubile high-school girls in a manner that would not survive in today's legal and social standards.

"How do you feel today?" he would ask his chesty teaching assistant *du jour*.

"Oh, fine, I guess," she would typically respond.

"Oh, I'll bet you do!" he would chortle. The students would laugh along and the assistant would blush. It's amazing to recall now that people once got away with such public behavior, especially around minors.

On this first morning of class, Mr. Crouch got on with the business of taking roll. He scanned the bosoms before him, then sat down at his desk, and whipped open his attendance book.

"Okay, what've we got this year…? Allen, Kirsten. Here?"

"Here."

"All right. Anderson, James."

"Here."

"Okay. Uh, hmm. Hell. This can't be a real name. Squib? Is there a Squib here???"

The students in the room fell to pieces. They rolled in the aisles, clutching their sides. I blushed in the back row. I raised my hand sheepishly and tried to blurt out, after the din subsided, "Uh, I go by Robbie."

Mr. Crouch was nothing if not sympathetic. "Whew! Well, that's a good thing!" This prompted another outpouring of hoots from my classmates.

It wasn't till I reached my mid-30s that I became comfortable telling people about my real name and being able to joke about it. But life grew much easier once I finally reached that milestone.

A balanced view of world history is good for an immigrant's self-esteem

The flights to and from Islamabad were grueling. About 10 1/2 hours straight to London, a five-hour layover there, then another eight and a half hours to Pakistan. You would arrive in Islamabad at 5:45 a.m. local time, feeling disoriented, and collapse for a six-hour nap characterized by a purest possible sense of unconsciousness.

On the way back, you would stop in London and have the chance to stay overnight. I adored those layovers, taking the above-ground portion of Underground from Heathrow Airport past those quaint British suburbs, wandering around Piccadilly Circus, and absorbing the rich energy of England. I was an Anglophile, fascinated by the nation that seemed the true motherland of my true American home. I never felt so Western as when I basked ever-so-briefly in the English countryside. It was like something out of Tolkien. Or vice versa. But either way, it was transcendent.

Yet I never seemed to spend more than 12 or 14 hours there, due to lacking funds that could have allowed for a longer stay. As I approached the age of 40 years later, I at last decided to set aside enough money to see my favorite place three times over the course of two years. I went to the British Museum twice as an adult, and I was struck to see first-hand the manner in which Egyptian and Chinese and Indus Valley and Assyrian civilizations were so much more advanced than the West for so much of human history. A trip to the Museum of London showed that, thousands of years after those groups were shaping society, Englishmen were living in a sub-hillbilly style.

I'd heard all the "left-wing propaganda" about the relevance and majesty of non-Western achievements, but I mostly dismissed it as an obsession of white liberals and minorities who bonded on the basis of their wishful thinking. Even if China and Egypt and Pakistan-India had heydays, I reasoned that the West was the civilization that most steadily cruised toward progress. It just seemed "superior." And I was haunted by the sense that the blood that ran through my veins was irrevocably "other."

But it was on my later visits to London, and in recent readings of people like Bernard Lewis, that I came to realize what a shocking and recent development it was for the West to suddenly leap past the rest of the world in terms of what we consider societal progress. Had I known as a child what I know now, I might not have grown up feeling quite so inadequately "other."

Sex, booze and bad traffic: You learn a lot about a society from the form of chaos it most dreads

Alcohol and sex are symbols of chaos for fundamentalists, whether in Pakistan or America. The difference is that most Americans tell Gallup that they sort of believe in God without sweating the details, while most Pakistanis are fundamentalists. Bear in mind that there's still a big difference between a fundamentalist and an extremist. Sure, an American "fundie" may whine about abortion or may forbid her son from parties or dancing or dating. (One of my favorite jokes is, "Why do Southern Baptists avoid premarital sex? Because it might lead to dancing.") But unless she bombs abortion clinics, she's just a fundie and *not* an extremist. And while all fundie Muslims will shun alcohol, they will not defend the killing of innocents in the alleged name of their religion.

Alcohol and sex symbolize a breakdown in the social order. The funny thing is that a Muslim country like Pakistan doesn't have much order anyway—traffic is a nightmare, bribery is standard practice, you can pay off someone easily if you accidentally ran over their first-born child or their brother, and litter and refuse are year-round decorations. But if you sip some chardonnay or look longingly into a girl's eyes, you've shredded the fabric of their society.

In America, it's the reverse. Traffic is orderly. You get honked at if you dare move too far to the side of your lane—and a honk is an affront here, whereas it's just a way to signal your presence in Pakistan. The American streets are regularly cleansed of human and animal waste. Bureaucracies run smoothly, and no one cuts in line at the post office. But drunkenness is often celebrated and premarital hand-holding is oftentimes condoned.

These are different societies with different tolerances for chaos. You learn a lot about a person or a society from which kinds of chaos they let slide and which ones they avoid.

But best understood, Pakistan and America aren't polar opposites, they're just spots on a spectrum. America's puritanical DNA makes it halfway between Pakistan and Europe. The Pakistanis don't "hate our freedoms" as much as the Europeans laugh at our puritanical rigidity, because Europe doesn't have any fundamentalists. (They don't have any fundies who run the society, anyway. And there are good reasons to believe that the "Eurabia" panic is overstated, as Philip Jenkins showed us in *God's Continent).*

Blondie's not so slutty after all

When Allah wasn't personally available to warn me about the evils of fleshly pleasure, he delegated the task to Dad, his loyal and eager deputy.

While perusing the comics section one evening as a 10 year-old, I found myself catching up on the antics of Dagwood Bumstead, who knew how to make one helluva large sandwich, yet who had the misfortune of having his comic-strip named for his wife, Blondie.

I asked my parents, "Say, what kind of name is 'Blondie'?"

Dad turned from the evening sitcoms and said, "Blondie? That is a word for a woman who is a… tramp."

"Huh?"

"Yes. Some loose girl who will run around with everybody." Mom nodded in mild agreement.

Color me befuddled. How could this be? Blondie seemed every bit as faithfully monogamous as Mom, at least in the strips that I read. Brenda Starr, now she seemed like a whore. But then again, who knows what Mary Worth and Blondie did after-hours…? Blondie did seem like quite a hot little thing, much like the secretary in Sad Sack comics. Maybe the artists were hiding something.

• • • • • • • •

We watched *Family Feud* one night, during which Richard Dawson would make shameless love to whatever woman appeared as a guest on the show. Little Ferhan, nine years younger than I and more conservative, would usually avert his eyes when that pig Dawson would peck a woman on the lips.

One young woman was wearing a tube top, in keeping with the zeitgeist. "That whore," Dad mumbled under his breath.

"What? I think she looks pretty good," I said. But Dad came from a village where even today many women feel trashy if they wear short sleeves in public.

• • • • • • •

"We want our children to have the best of both worlds," Dad would always say. "We want them to have the best of the East and the best of the West." That was code for wanting us to be as successful as Americans but as pious as Pakistanis. No boozing, no whoring.

And he knew this was possible for his "three tigers," because we were, well, not three tigresses. "If we had three daughters, we would have moved back to Pakistan," he once said. So much for his bold American journey. It was just luck that kept him in America.

But his view was that an indiscretion on the part of a son was manageable. But an indiscretion on the part of a daughter would ruin the family.

On segregating the sexes: There are rooms, very exciting rooms, out there somewhere

By the time I was a college student at USC, I had grown skeptical of religious morality, of the notion that a noisy God upstairs was threatening, "Don't make me come down there." But Dad eagerly filled in during Allah's many pauses and silences.

Dad would insist that religious rules were there for the sake of social decency and order. You had to keep women dressed modestly, and keep them at a distance.

"If you put a man in a room alone with a woman…." he observed coolly, "….the chances are they will end up having sex."

It was that simple and that convenient? I wanted to ask, "Wait, where exactly are these rooms?" But I bit my tongue.

But I did say, "Dad, there are lots of times that guys are in rooms alone with women, and sex doesn't happen, no matter how much the guy tries."

"Well, when they're drinking, it happens."

Again, I wondered why this alcohol+opposite sex recipe had yielded so little results to that point for my freshman friends and me. Was Dad exaggerating to make his point, or was I just really inept? In his defense, the recipe worked far better on fraternity row, although I believe the guys there had a coolness, a wardrobe and a social status that was at least as productive as the alcohol.

• • • • • • •

The clash of secular and traditional civilizations isn't at its most pitched in the area of governance approaches or concepts of international cooperation. The biggest tension involves how to act—well, sex, really. This is borne out over and over in surveys of Muslim and Western nations. It's borne out when ultra-orthodox Jews deface a billboard of a scantily clad woman in Tel Aviv, or when they attack a woman for daring to expose her arms in a conservative part of Jerusalem. It's borne out by the Christian governors from Alaska who oppose sex education even though they know it increases the chance their daughters will get knocked up. Yeah, it's the sex that really worries the traditionalists. They'd normally all be on the same side, fighting the porno-loving secular fornicators, if they didn't get distracted by whether Jerusalem should remain the undivided capital of Israel.

As for Dad, I resisted telling him my opinion that conservative religious people who frowned upon sex were unwittingly showing us a lot about their own inner life.

Many religious men are like every other guy; left to themselves, they would try to nail any woman they could. But religious men prefer to erect barriers that keep them out of trouble rather than to allow a free society in which people can choose to do as they please, with all the spontaneous goodness and all the dangers that could come from such an arrangement. It also allows them to believe that they'd be Casanovas if only the Lord permitted it, rather than confronting the bloody truth that they wouldn't be that good at bedding the average woman.

The Bee Gees were evil, but you knew that

As a sixth-grader in northern Virginia, I stepped to the front lines of the clash between God's People and Satan's Perverts.

My senses were assaulted once I turned 11 at Fairhill Elementary School. My classmates' minds dripped with sex, oozed sex, and spoke sex, in ways that left me a constant blush.

My male peers lobbed dirty jokes at one another across the lunch table, and then looked at me in puzzlement as I looked at them in puzzlement. I was less offended than I was confused. Jokes about a woman turning on her headlights because a snake was in her bush; references to mysterious biological processes; something about buttered popcorn. Huh?

One classmate, Jim, had a reckless imagination but no prospects because he was a dork, which seemed to fuel his imagination even more. Once, after quizzing me about the extent of my sexual knowledge, which I resisted, he looked at the others and laughed, "Geez, this dude's as clean as a plate!" I took it as a compliment.

• • • • • • •

A few days later, a record store was giving away album covers. Not vinyl records, just covers. As a 12-year-old of modest means, I thought this was a decent step toward increasing my music library, so I eagerly sifted through the bin. I came across a cover for *Main Course*, a Bee Gees album—my favorite band at that moment in time.

On it was a cartoon of a shapely nude woman bathing in a teaspoon. I'm not sure if she was a small nude woman in a normal-sized teaspoon or a normal-sized nude woman in a large teaspoon. But what's pertinent is that she was stark naked, except for a dainty straw hat that topped her angelic head.

This posed a dilemma. I loved the Bee Gees, and I prized that album cover for reasons that no longer seem clear; but I couldn't bring that decadence into my family's house, could I?

I could. I was bold. I picked up a couple of other album covers with which to sandwich it, asked for a bag for my empty covers, which struck the saleswoman as an odd request, and managed to get them home without attracting the concern of my parents or God above.

Sometime later, Pawan, a large-eared classmate from India who lived down the street, was visiting my house. I furtively pulled out the *Main Course* cover and gigglingly showed the bathing beauty to him.

"So?" he asked.

"She's naked!"

"Geez. It's just a *cartoon*, Rob."

"Um," I muttered. "Yeah. I know that." Chastened by my South-Asian buddy, I put the album cover away and realized that my standards and the prevailing culture's standards were separated by more than an ocean.

And let me remind you, not so long after the controversy over Danish depictions of the Prophet, that cartoons can indeed be a big deal.

· · · · · · ·

Not long after the cartoon decadence, I visited the house of another friend, Tom. Tom was a nerdish, bookish boy who became a friend to me, because, like me, he found friends hard to come by and at this point we were both willing to lower our expectations, cut our losses, and be seen in the lunchroom together. I received permission from Mom to visit him after school one afternoon, and we spent most of that time watching television.

While I was on the phone to update Mom about when I'd be home for dinner, Tom sneaked out his father's Playboy collection, a substantial one, and proceeded to pull various issues open to the centerfold and push them into my face while giggling like Beavis. I did my best not to cry out for help, because Mom would never let me visit him again if she knew what he was doing as I spoke to her.

But in truth, I had an active imagination, which didn't even require pornography for fueling. One afternoon that imagination seemed to engage me and my classmate Susan on a cruise ship—this was probably an inevitable fantasy, due to how much we watched *The Love Boat* at the time. My conservative family loved the show. (I was thrilled to run into Gopher years later in an elevator on Capitol Hill after he had been elected a congressman from Iowa).

After I entertained this fantasy in more vivid and longer-lasting ways than normal for me, I was horrified to see a nasty electrical storm roll into Springfield late that night. Crashing and bullying thunder. Spider webs of crackling lightning. Driving winds. The Cosmic Spoilsport had ridden into town to punish me. I sat in bed and prayed that He would spare me just this one time, and that I would not trouble Him any further with any naughtiness. Boy, did other people have to suffer through quite a storm just so God could make his point to me. In any event, the fantasies revved up again with the next day's first sunlight, as did the guilt.

Hindus get the ladies

Hindus can be extremely conservative culturally, but they can still mesh with Western values more easily than do typical Muslims.

During my family's treks to the motherland, I found that Indians (90% of whom are Hindu) were fierce rivals of Pakistanis (97% of whom are Muslim), but those saucy Indian Bollywood movies have been a big hit in Pakistan nonetheless – much bigger than Pakistan's own Lollywood movies (Bollywood was named for the Indian film capital of Bombay, a.k.a. Mumbai, while Lollywood was named for Lahore, Mom's hometown). While both societies have been sexually conservative traditionally, Bollywood has consistently been willing to push the envelope more than Lollywood.

As a teenager, I watched a *60 Minutes* feature on Bollywood, which noted that there are two kinds of Indian movies: Bad ones and really bad ones.

These movies overflowed with frolic and fun. Indian actresses dressed provocatively, while men tripped over one another in hot pursuit. All of them broke into song at random moments to express joy at having experienced love and sorrow at the fact that their parents forbade their love on account of class or caste. A good majority of Pakistani Muslims (as well as more traditional Hindus) would watch these movies the way a Midwestern American homemaker might—shaking their titillated heads in enthusiastic disapproval.

Willa Cather once observed, "There are only two or three human stories, and they go on repeating themselves as fiercely as if they had never happened before." Had she lived in India, she might have revised the number downward.

But the Bollywood movies are said to be growing up, though I keep my watching of them to an absolute curious minimum. In recent years, *Salaam Namaste* dealt with pregnancy out of wedlock and abortion, while *Dostana* had a *Three's Company* gag plot about two Indian guys in Miami who pretend to be a gay couple so they can shack up with a beautiful Indian woman. That's scandalous in traditional Indian society, and even more scandalous in Pakistan.

When Richard Gere planted a long, "vulgar" kiss on Indian actress Shilpa Shetty, protesters burned him in effigy while chanting "Death to Shilpa Shetty." It reminds us that we shouldn't overestimate the difference between Hindus and Muslim, and that "Death to fill-in-the-blank" rolls quite easily off the tongues of people in that part of the world, and that maybe we shouldn't take it too personally.

But all things considered, India's Hindu majority has traditions of Kama Sutra sexuality and a pelvis-centric dancing style that would scandalize most middle-Americans this side of Elvis. Most Hindus enjoy a more elastic moral code than Pakistan's Muslim majority. Hindus can drink, gamble and wear skirts. Muslims cannot—and if you see a Muslim doing so, she is praying that you will not tag her on Facebook with the cell phone pictures you just took.

Romance is the great struggle for Christian singles in the 21st century
Adam Carolla, the former co-host of *Loveline* and a gifted student of the human condition, once observed, "Men don't want to get married. They'd be happy to have a girlfriend for a hundred years. If a guy really wants to get married, that's a warning sign that something's wrong."

Indeed, "the world" would see such a person as needy or lacking better prospects. But for us guys in church, marriage represented the only way we could get laid.

So we desperately sought marriage because we desperately sought sex. The problem was that we were living in an age when women could provide for themselves, so they could afford to be pickier about whom they would marry (and women weren't as desperate to have sex as guys were anyway). God hadn't seemed to catch up to the times. Christian couples paired off less often than they did in past years within churches, and did so at much later ages if at all.

The members of the BRICK young adults group from church had many discussions about "nice guys" and "bad boys." Christian men naturally fell into the nice guy category, and often brooded about whether they were missing out on romantic successes that bad boys could achieve. It didn't help that the best "catches" in BRICK seemed most attracted to neurotic types. Were we really "new creations" who lived in the light, to use the Apostle Paul's terms, or were we just hairless chimpanzees who overdressed our animal behavior in lofty terms?

• • • • • • •

In 2001, at a lush and scenic Christian conference center south of Santa Barbara at which BRICK held its annual summer retreat, I was formally installed, for the second time, as BRICK's president, which required a great deal of patience dealing with people who expected church to feel like heaven.

I carpooled back from the retreat with a close friend, Joanne, a bright, married woman who was training at Fuller Seminary to become a marital therapist. Comparing me to Matt, my good friend and predecessor as president, Joanne remarked on his charming presence. She mused, "A tall, warm guy like Matt sure is able to fill up the room."

I was 5-foot-7, not a dwarf, but a little on the compact side. And her comment rattled me. I had recently been attempting Internet dating, only to find that most women detailed a preference for "tall, successful, handsome men"—with "tall" consistently being the first preference, and Caucasian being a "read between the lines" preference for many women and an explicit preference for others. Before these experiences, I had never conceived of height as an issue, since I was at least as tall as most women to whom I was attracted. But suddenly I was reading online profiles by 5-foot-2 women who expected suitors to be at least 5-foot-11.

Still puzzling over Joanne's remark, I pulled into a Wendy's restaurant so that we could grab a quick bite to eat before continuing our journey back to L.A. But as we got back on the road, I couldn't resist bringing up Joanne's remark.

"It's funny that you mentioned the height issue," I said. "I've actually been finding on the Internet dating sites that women seem to really like tall men."

"Yeah," she said matter-of-factly. "I think it's biological."

I was crestfallen. She was right, I knew it, but I hated the idea that biology—in the form of height or race—would be such a factor in mate selection. Wasn't a living, loving God more likely to orchestrate mating selection than was cold biology? That notion was foundational to my personal hopes and my faith, but it was becoming less plausible with each passing year.

I eventually wondered if I had subconsciously been hoping that Christian faith would give me the DNA of true Americana and the ability to fit in. It didn't.

The family of Altaf, my Bizarro-world Canadian friend, had insisted that I wouldn't be able to get happily married in America because of the color of my skin. I scoffed at their biological fatalism. And yet I was still single, and when intelligent friends commiserated with me on why such-and-such woman rebuffed me despite her seeming compatibility, they would admit that race could have been a factor. I didn't see this as a marital death-sentence, given that I knew many Asians who married whites and Hispanics who married Asians and what not. I believed that race was less of a factor than my own personal hangups, which I had committed to addressing through rigorous self-analysis.

Just the same, I wondered why dating was such a struggle.

• • • • • • •

All things sexual were a struggle for young and no-longer-young Christians who were actively involved in church.

Waiting for God to deliver a girlfriend or boyfriend was a struggle. Trying to stay chaste with said friend was a struggle. Refraining from masturbation was a struggle for them too. Our psychologist-pastor Laura once lectured to our BRICK group that masturbation isn't necessarily a sin as long as you can keep from imagining an actual partner. Easy for Laura to say, she wasn't a hyper-visual male. Yet that almost produced a riot in the group, with members protesting that she was promoting evil.

In truth, all the guys I knew in BRICK admitted that they masturbated regularly, but they felt terrible about it and prayed for forgiveness constantly. Contrast this with "The Contest" on *Seinfeld*: What was a routine bodily function for mainstream society was a traumatizing compulsion for single Christians.

No wonder most of them got married too early, and the rest of the confused lot got married too late or not at all. We usually had naïve views, too, about how fulfilling their sex lives would be if they just "waited" until marriage. Unfortunately, many in my church crowd didn't wait for marriage; they rushed into it, and then found that their human foibles or repressed libidos kept them from having great sex.

Meanwhile the secular crowd seemed to be able to get over themselves nicely. Some got pregnant unintentionally, granted, but most seemed to be able to get laid on occasion without having their heads or hearts explode. Many joked about how often they'd gratify themselves, and they didn't go blind.

They weren't struggling, and as I noticed this, I myself found less able to take the judgmental view that they were merely "fallen" people stumbling in the dark. They increasingly seemed better-adjusted than we Christians. It moved me onto a different path eventually.

Repress sex and it will eventually come out of your ears

Shabi had noticed an odd thing in Islamabad 30 years ago, when he was a teen-ager: Pakistani male teens and young men had a tendency to hold hands as they walked down the street. Mom insisted it wasn't an indication of what he thought it was, but Shabi was convinced that men holding men's hands was a sexualized expression of friendship within a society where you couldn't easily get your hands on women.

That made sense to me. Years later in church, I noticed that the most romantically frustrated young women tended to play with one another's hair compulsively; they couldn't keep their hands off each other. And many single church women and men loved swing dancing, as noted earlier (we weren't as strict as the Southern Baptists in this regard). When I mentioned to my friend Sam that swing dancing had become his obsession because it was the closest he would get to getting laid in the near future, he scoffed at the idea. I asked him if he'd dance as often if it were something you do with members of your own sex, as happens in some cultures. He called that a nonsensical point.

But I felt I'd made a good point nonetheless. Religious young men and women were glib in word and action about how they "sought to honor the Lord" with their bodies. They didn't often understand the ramifications and the inconsistencies involved. It increasingly made sense that a psychologically healthy approach to sexuality would involve something beyond the rigid "no premarital sex" edicts of church.

·· ·· ·· ··

The avoidance of premarital sex at times could be pernicious. People didn't marry within a few years of puberty anymore due to career obligations—and considering that the hormones in food now brought the onset of puberty down to the age of, oh, nine or so, a religious person could easily go some three decades without sex.

Within a highly sexualized society, one result was that evangelical singles tended to play Clintonian games with the definition of sex. Many of them believed that everything short of intercourse was fair game within a dating relationship, including staying over at the other's house.

I mentioned to some friends that the typical, conservative Muslim—or a Christian from a more conservative era—would see that as silly hairsplitting, and that such a person would tell them to just strap on a condom at that point and finish the deed. But they derived a particular satisfaction from saving something for marriage—which they rushed into nonetheless, often with disastrous consequences.

Certain aspects of traditional religious morality are founded on sound enough principles of integrity and restraint. Yet conservative religious figures evaporated their credibility through a fixation on reductionist approaches to sexuality. Concepts such as sex are handled with obsessive tones that undercut any effort to promote responsible living. The best psychologists will agree that certain forms of sexual "acting out" can cause harm, but they can't take the black-and-white, angel-and-demon approach of religious conservatives.

A black comedy of Christian dating— or, how saving the world won't get you laid

Compatibility, not chemistry, has generally been the core issue in arranged marriages. Compatibility of families, compatibility of values, compatibility of financial interests and so on.

And the notion that compatibility came first left an impression on me within the world of church dating, as I believed for years that women didn't crave unbridled romance as much as they craved friendship that could later blossom into romance. I believed that most American men rudely treated women as sexual objects, much to women's chagrin, and that women would respond to someone who treated them with platonic respect by offering their fullest romantic affection.

With this in mind, I attempted to use an uncommon blend of niceness and craftiness in my own romantic mis-exploits during my church days. Step 1 involved waiting till a woman caught my eye. Step 2 involved spending three or four months discerning in Mr. Spock-like fashion whether the female specimen in question was compatible with me and whether any ethical issues prevented me from expressing immediate interest.

If I decided the woman was compatible and that it was appropriate to move forward, I moved to Step 3 and proceeded to surreptitiously woo her with an abundance of generosity and friendship, planning to introduce romantic feelings only after some six months had passed. The woman typically would wind up engaged to someone else by the second or third month, and I would go back to Step 1.

Step 1 and Step 2 played out predictably when I met Kate, a perky blonde who began attending the BRICK group in the mid-90s. I was now almost 30, and she was 25. A native of semi-rural Modesto, California, she was a proud USC Trojan, like me. I was immediately smitten. Could it be destiny....? She seemed to be the embodiment of the all-American girl, a girl who came from a different, cleaner, brighter, better-smelling dimension than I.

Kate ended up dating someone else while I was waiting out the usual six-month time period. It gave me hope when she finally dumped the creep, who was loved by Jesus but by no one else as far as I could tell, but what ensued was more haplessness in which I kept hope alive even though she claimed she wasn't ready to date. But she was ready to request, and receive, my constant attentions and eager support for her musings and her missions projects to save the children of the world. With a zesty mix of genuine enthusiasm, self-delusion and self-interest, I became her church missions sidekick: I hosted missions-planning meetings at my apartment (some of the rare occasions on which I was willing to cook), I helped organize trips to an orphanage in Mexico, I joined the church's missions committee to lobby on her behalf, and I used my clout with the new pastor to get him to promote a missions class that she and I spent months organizing.

When Dean, the director of the Mexican orphanage came to speak to BRICK one Sunday, he asked us to consider committing to spending one year overseas on a mission at some point in our lives. He then called us forward if we would commit. I joined about 10 of my peers up there. Dean prayed to God for protection and strength for us stalwarts. This would prove to Kate that I was committed to the things she was committed to.

Oddly, stunningly, Kate didn't come forward herself to make such a commitment. Within a year or two, she went on to marry a wealthy buddy of mine, settle into a Southern California suburb, and have two children. She retired from work and tended happily to her all-American family.

And I was on the hook for a one-year trip overseas. I'd made a vow before my God and my church. Fortunately, I would later run out on them both. But I did have to live with various consequences that resulted from opening up the Pandora's jar of missions.

• • • • • • •

In the wake of my foiled attempts to grab the brass ring from Kate's chest or to grab Kate's chest like a brass ring, I met Karey, a cheerful redheaded, "on-fire" Christian from Texas. Karey swooped into my heart one day when she came in from Houston to be a bridesmaid in a wedding party for which I was a groomsman. We made a handsome couple, I thought, walking arm-in-arm down the aisle, she in a sunshiney yellow dress and me in a far-too-tight tuxedo from my college days.

Karey was a natural evangelizer. She took courses on it at Oxford and she became a full-time minister. "I just want to reach the lost and tell them that Jesus loves them," she said with utter sincerity. I was built differently. I had convinced myself of evangelicalism's rightness, but I was far more aware of the difficulties of cramming one's own beliefs down the throat of the world. We evangelicals led peculiar lives. Our pastors cajoled us to "witness" to our work colleagues and our neighbors. To invite them for cookies, and then snare them into Bible studies, all so that we could save souls. Karey was built for that, and I wasn't. I suspect it was good we didn't end up together, especially in light of how things changed from there.

I sometimes felt a pressure to be a great evangelizer. Being stuck on missions committees, which was partly due to my previous crush on Kate, tended to add to the pressure. My Muslim background added to the pressure; many church people prized the notion of having claimed a Muslim, and their ambition was for me to be "fruitful."

Given my caution, my tendency to see the world in shades of gray rather than black-and-white, and my desire to show respect to my family, I was more than a little subtle about evangelism. Also, I had relatives in another part of the U.S. who I sometimes felt were militant enough to hurt me if they discovered my religious affiliations.

Karey shared something surprising one day over lunch. "You know, I had the strangest dream last night. You and I were getting married…"

My eyebrow arched heavenward at this point.

"…And I told you, Rob, if you don't want to get married in a church and use Christian vows to keep your family happy, I'll understand. But you said, 'No, no, we'll do it in a Christian way. And I was so impressed with your strength. So anyway, the wedding day comes and I'm walking up the aisle, when someone shoots me."

"What?"

"Someone shot me. It was a relative of yours who was mad about the whole thing, and he shot me in the head!"

"Wow. I'm sorry to make you go through that, Karey."

"Well, it really didn't hurt. I just stood there and said, 'Hey, I've been shot in the head.'"

I smiled. The story revealed the undercurrents of our platonic relationship, which I was too hesitant to advance to a romantic level for good and bad reasons, but it also showed Karey "got" it: For a Christian woman to marry me would involve a taking up of a larger cross than the one you'd take up in marrying some white guy who believed in Jesus just because he grew up that way.

The patriarchs fear nothing more than a strong woman

"Males have authority over women because the Lord created one above the other, and because man provides for the woman."

—Quran, 4:34

Mom graduated from her housewife position in 1978, when she and Dad bought a commercial lot in then-new Islamabad on which they'd erect a five-story office building. Dad had to take a high-paying telecommunications job in Sudan to fund it, and Mom had to direct the contractors, architects and laborers.

That's when I first realized that patriarchal societies are paper tigers.

Mom would walk into a bank, see a line of 60 bearded patriarchs waiting patiently, thunder her way to the front of the line and start yelling at the clerk. A manager in a suit and tie would scamper over to help her. No one complained—no one would dare. But if any male below the rank of a senator attempted that, he'd be tossed out on his ear.

That was my epiphany: Patriarchal cultures are patriarchies precisely because men in those cultures are scared of women and need to set up rules to keep them in check. They do this for women's, uh, "protection," and many women claim this is a good thing (including Mom). But Mom also adjusted her game accordingly when she needed to get things done, using the leverage of being attractive and refined.

• • • • • • •

Most religious men—from *every* religion—tend to be a bit terrified of the power of a woman's sexuality. Religion is a terrific way to get the gods on your side. Whenever you see a deeply conservative religious man talking about how women should be submissive to men, you get the sense that he's downright terrified of what the fairer sex would do if she got a little education and a little authority.

Richard Dawkins, in *The God Delusion*, argued that the God of the Old Testament revealed the psychological projection of jealous husbands worrying about their wives' infidelity.

It makes sense. In the Bible, God is constantly lamenting how his Israel is an unfaithful slut (a "Blondie"?). He's regularly comparing his chosen people in Israel to wives who run off to become prostitutes, due to their "lust" for lovers with "horse-sized" genitalia. Today, we wince at the Almighty's shallow view of the motivations behind prostitution, and apologists would explain that He only sounds insecure because we don't properly understand divine or ancient ways.

So again, a religious conservative would say, "These rules are just in place because male sexual power is the real worry—and that the scarves, veils, burqas and isolation are inventions to keep women out of the way of men's reckless penises.

I still think there's fear involved. A guy who thinks he can compete in the sexual marketplace says, "Set the women free! Let's see where they go and who they'll do!" A guy who fears he's a geek who can't get or keep women will say, "No, they need to stay at home, where they'll be safe from, um, *our* reckless sexuality."

Um, yeah, sure. That's why they prescribe female circumcision in places such as Egypt. They say they're relieving young women of the complications of sexuality, but they're really robbing young women of sexual pleasure in hopes that they won't stray toward greener sexual pastures.

• • • • • • • •

As an adult, I was never was able to convince Mom that she was oppressed, though I did my damndest. She scoffed at the charge, certain that she lacked nothing as a Muslim woman. She rather felt liberated from what she saw as impossible Western pressures on women to create public images that turned themselves into mere slabs of flesh.

Dad did feel, though, that Mom had been ruined by those soap operas on American TV, giving her those lousy ideas about being independent and liberated.

Most Pakistani women, though, are like Mom. They don't worry much about the strict laws and conservative interpretations that give them less power than men. And those who do worry about it are outnumbered in a large way.

But again, Mom and many other women know how to manage in such societies. During my visit to Islamabad in 1998, for Ferhan's wedding, I sat around our parents' house and watched my aunts gab about life. When their husbands dropped in later in the day, the men dutifully took orders from the women about which errands to run and when to breathe and when to sit. In a patriarchal society, women had an unusual amount of power—just not in the ways that we in the West would want or expect. Women could run their nuclear and extended families; they could micromanage the lives of their adult sons and daughters-in-law and grandchildren; they could be waited on hand and foot. Some would say patriarchy is a bargain in that context.

Eat, drink, but don't be merry

If Muslims and Pat Robertson can agree about one thing, it's that America is a Christian nation.

Both will argue this against any secular humanist who dares suggest otherwise. The stereotype among Pakistani Muslims is that all Americans are more or less Christian, and that Christians are decent people who are, well, a bit lazy. Christians in this view practice "religion lite," giving themselves an easy route to heaven that involves alcohol and all the uncertainty that alcohol unleashes. It is all a tad too easy and convenient, many Muslims suspect. Even the Quran promises that those who resist temptation on earth will recline in paradise besides streams of "non-intoxicating wine," which would have to have a really, *really* good nose and finish to be worth the trouble.

• • • • • • •

Dad, Shabi and I popped into a suburban California restaurant one night for dinner when I was 15. A waitress dropped by and welcomed us warmly.

"Good evening, how are all of you?" she asked.

"We are fine," said Dad. "Thank you."

"Sir," she said to Dad, "Can I get you started with a cocktail?"

"Sssssssss….. Oh, my. No, no, no. No cocktails! Thank you. No! We do *not* drink."

"Oh. Uh, okay. I'll be back in a minute for your order."

Shabi later looked annoyed, "Boy, Dad, it was like you were a tire that went flat. 'Sssssssssssssssssssssss……….' You could have just said, 'Thank you, I will just have a Coke.'"

Dad coolly pulled the trigger on his usual response: "Shut up."

For his part, Dad wasn't trying to act morally superior to the waitress, even if he knew he was superior to that bare-shouldered hussy. He was simply showing a natural reaction to something he had been raised to detest.

As much as Dad loved his adopted home of America, he was disturbed by drinking. "I tell you," he would say, "this alcohol will cause the downfall of America and the West."

"They've been doing it for a lot of centuries, Dad, and America's still kicking the rest of the world's butts," I'd respond. "How long is this downfall supposed to take?"

While inculcating in us an anti-alcohol attitude when we were a few years younger, Dad told Shabi and me the story of some old Hindu college roommates who had a vice or two.

"They loved to drink beer," he said. "Their fridge was full of it. One day, we decided to play a trick on them. We emptied out their bottles and... we peed in them. And those bastards didn't know the difference."

I shook my head and chuckled. Those Hindus were silly. Years later, I wondered why Dad had to concoct that absurdity. But years later still, I found that many Indians indeed swear by "urine therapy." I think Dad chose to weave that into his own myth of nutty people who will drink whatever evil is plunked down in front of them.

Oh, hell, just be merry

As a surreptitious drinker, I wished I could get Dad to relax and enjoy a drink. Or at least watch me have a cold beer or two while playing him in chess; that way he could personally witness that I could still coolly checkmate him as I normally did, rather than my morphing into some raging maniac who would sweep aside the chess pieces and seduce him.

To paraphrase the old soda jingle, I'd like to teach the world to drink, in perfect harmony. That includes Muslims in my family's native Pakistan and freshmen at American colleges. I'd like Amir to taste the simple sophistication of a gin and tonic. And I'd like Biff to learn to appreciate the differences between a merlot and a zinfandel.

About 100 college presidents, from such institutions as Tufts, the University of Massachusetts, Dartmouth and Duke, signed an Amethyst Initiative petition in 2008 calling for lowering the drinking age nationally. They were greeted as barbarians by many outraged parents and social workers. That's because Americans have a view of alcohol surprisingly similar to that of much of the Muslim world. Europeans see drinking as natural. Americans and Muslims see it as naughty. The difference between America and Muslim nations is that America lets its citizens give expression to their naughtiness; Muslims don't. (Although, even America tried to take the right to drink away in the time of Puritan zeal called Prohibition).

If you've ever taken a Western airline out of Pakistan, you've noticed that, as the airplane reaches cruising altitude, a good many Pakistanis shed façades and order up wine and cocktails with their in-flight meals, often buying copious amounts of duty-free vodka for good measure. They're liberal enough to believe that God forbids over-the-top drunkenness, not every last sip of one of humanity's most poetic achievements.

But over-the-top drinking is a real risk for those of us who achieve escape velocity from teetotalling mores. I found that out in my own college days, to Dad's horror.

After college and after years of avoiding any alcohol, one glass of cabernet sauvignon, in the company of friends during the holidays several years ago, ushered me into a new era with a new attitude toward the pleasures of "adult beverages," though I didn't bother telling Dad about this change of heart. Savoring the caramel wallop of dark rum, the liberating tang of a good margarita, or the sheer, over-sweetened fun of "girlie" fruit martinis stood in contrast to the macho but joyless romps of college days. All this, with no hangovers, no DUIs, no drama.

I'm sad that I still felt a need to hide my non-mayhemic, adult chapter of social drinking from my father. But it only would have kept him up at night, as all good parents of every age stay up when they worry for their progeny.

Still, I side with the college presidents who recommend a lower drinking age. A high drinking age—one that's delayed for five years past the age when you can drive and three years past the age when you can fight and die for your country—magnifies the sense that alcohol is a naughty substance.

Many European parents teach their children in their early teen years, in small doses, to appreciate some wine with their dinner. One key result, as marketing expert Clotaire Rapaille noted in *The Culture Code*, is that alcohol there lacks the subversive, violent thrill that it holds in America. Let's face it, nothing is more uncool than what Mom and Pop teach you to enjoy.

So the paradox is that if those who fear alcohol's adverse affects could step back and allow their societies to embrace the positive aspects of alcohol, alcohol's adverse effects would diminish greatly.

Now wouldn't that be worth a toast?

Help others to shine, and you'll shine

Warren Bennis, the great leadership guru who wrote this book's foreword and for whom I served for several years as an editor, used to share a story about the noted 19th century British prime ministers William Gladstone and Benjamin Disraeli to teach a lesson about what distinguishes a great leader from a good leader. Bennis would note that, when you went to dinner with Gladstone, you walked away thinking, "That William Gladstone is the wittiest, the most intelligent, the most charming person around." However, when you went to dinner with Benjamin Disraeli, you walked away thinking, "I'm the wittiest, the most intelligent, the most charming person around."

To Bennis, Disraeli was the greater leader, because he used his standing to help those around him to shine. When a prime minister of what was the world's greatest nation believes that you are a wonderful person, you feel like a wonderful person. When the prime minister is intent on getting himself praised as a wonderful person, you may offer that praise, but you are no richer for it. Disraeli could make others richer. In fact, he ultimately made himself richer for the bargain.

That philosophy appealed to me; it has eyes to see treasure where others see only barren land. It has eyes to see a saint where others see a sinner. It has eyes to see hope where others see despair.

Not everyone wanted to put up with me as a writer or a speaker. We lived in a consumer society, an entertainment culture, especially in Hollywood, and many people in my church always wanted "something better," a speaker who was more credentialed, more dynamic, more witty, more something than whatever they presently had. (And of course, some of them wanted someone who was more reflexively Bible-loving than I was). Some were brutally blunt about it, and it occasionally broke my confidence. But there were always others there to build me up, and it mattered. And it made me determined to build up other people.

Those who could come hear me speak, when I was still inexperienced and mumbly, were very rich people. They were able to find a gift in me and call it out. Those who could not suffer me, because they needed a more polished product, grew poorer. They could find speakers and experts and mentors and entertainers who momentarily met their expectations, but they could never be happy over the long haul. "Every hero becomes a bore at last," Emerson said. Those who divide the world into heroes and bores lose out. Those who look to find heroes buried inside each person are the ultimate winners.

I even was able to find treasures I had overlooked in my family. Recalling that Mom majored in fine arts at a Pakistani college, I encouraged her to take up painting for the first time in 40 years. After we took a trip to Aaron Brothers to pick up oils and canvases, she rolled up her sleeves and began churning out painting upon painting, all of excellent quality. Maria, Shabi, Pakeeza and I began putting them up on our walls, and they even passed the ultimate test of taste—Mom was willing to put them up in her own house.

A big area of growth was also to get over any bitterness about feeling that my parents had favored Shabi over me—the bitterness that made me unable at times to trust my own family. With the help of no small amount of therapy from my psychologist, Jim MacCuish, I could gradually come to see them for who they were—unusually loving and ever-present parents who did the best they could to care for me and prepare me for success based on their beliefs about what success looked like.

**There is a place where we are all equal,
though the sandwiches aren't cheap there**

Maybe the only place that felt like home was the airport. Any airport, in any city. I loved airports. They were the great equalizer. There, everyone was in flux, equally rootless. Nobody had a leg up on me, no one had home-field advantage. Here, *everyone* was somewhat out of place. I loved that level playing field. There, too, we would gaze upon and then board those 747s, those uniquely magnificent specimens of American ingenuity and "bigness."

Flight attendants would sometimes approach Shabi and me to tell us that the pilots wanted to give us a tour of the cockpit. I would shyly join Shabi and we would go up, get chatted up by the captains, and come back with coloring books and TWA or Pan Am badges. I don't suppose many Pakistani kids are invited up to the cockpit anymore. Heaven knows I'm not.

But maybe once a year I do still drop by Los Angeles International Airport's international terminal, to get some of that sense of permanent flux. And I try hard not to act suspicious. After paying $20 for a McDonald's combo, I head home, feeling fleeced but fulfilled.

Epilogue: Dad Didn't Make It Back (And I Nearly Didn't Either)

Dad gave his life for the school he built in his village, so that a thousand children would have easy access to quality education and to the manner of opportunity that would prevent extremism. He gave his life almost literally, spending much of his final years shuttling between Islamabad and the village, even though his health had been in steady decline. He'd soldiered through asthma for decades, but in his late 70s, he found it hard even to climb a flight of stairs without pausing halfway up.

I managed to fly to Pakistan to see Dad late in the spring of 2008, and it was my first opportunity to see his beloved school. I begged him not to put on a special event on account of my visit, but he couldn't resist. This school was his baby, and he desperately wanted me to appreciate it in the way that he did.

So the kids there put on a three-hour talent show on a muggy, 100-degree afternoon. A sign above the stage read, "In honor of Chairman Ali Asghar and his beloved son, Saqib Sohrab Asghar." Even Pakistanis can't seem to spell my name right, but it was still poignant for the "second worst man alive" to get such a reception at his father's school.

And yet I sensed I may be seeing him for the last time, such was his health. He claimed he'd come back soon to see Mom and us and his grandkids, who now totaled four—two from Ferhan and Pakeeza, and two from Shabi and Maria.

He then firmed up those plans, and I figured my fears were unfounded. I made plans to meet him at L.A. International Airport one Friday evening and drive him down to my parents' Orange County home.

Then the call came from my mother. Dad was dead. He had a heart attack on the leg of his journey from England to New York. By the time he reached the hospital, he couldn't be revived.

A shattered family collected him from New York and brought him to Orange County for a simple and fast burial according to Islamic custom. His grandkids struggled to understand what was happening. And we jumped on a plane to be with family in Pakistan. In his village. There, family and fellow villagers paid tribute to him profusely. He was an American and a Pakistani, and he embodied a generous and loving connection between these two strange worlds.

● ● ● ● ● ● ●

My front-row seat for the attacks on the American embassy and our American school in Islamabad in 1979 would be bracketed three decades later by another much-too-close anti-Western attack.

After returning from Dad's village to the home we kept in Islamabad—the home in which Dad spent his final weeks of life bedridden before deciding it was time to come back to the U.S.—Ferhan and I decided to run off and grab a quick dinner before a lawyer for my father would come by to discuss his last will and testament. Ferhan and I and his teen-aged brother in law Ali drove off toward the fancy Dynasty Chinese restaurant in the Islamabad Marriott, ignoring the pleas of Ferhan's wife Pakeeza, who hated the idea of our enjoying Dynasty's fine cuisine on an evening on which she was too busy to join us.

I may have felt guilty in going to Dynasty without her, but mostly I just felt cheap. Dynasty had seemed a bit overrated—and quite overpriced—on a visit the previous spring. "Hey, Ferhan," I said, "Why don't we go to some closer [read: cheaper] Chinese restaurant, and we can go with Pakeeza to Dynasty some other night?"

"Good point," he said. "Ali, is there some other place around here we can go to?"

"Well, there's the Golden Dragon at the Faisal market," Ali responded.

"Sounds great!" I said. And it sounded inexpensive, too.

As we dined at the cheaper restaurant, we heard an explosion. We wondered if a nearby embassy had been bombed.

As we would find out moments later through other diners' cellphones, the bombing took place at none other than the Marriott and its Dynasty restaurant: Some 60 people died that night, and another 270 were injured in an apparent attempt by the Taliban to send a message to Western tourists and expats and Westernized Pakistanis.

Given how Dynasty was located directly in front of where a truck containing 1,500 pounds of explosives had detonated, we'd most likely have been killed by jihadists. The war on terror had become personal.

Ferhan called Pakeeza to tell her we hadn't gone to the Marriott.

We returned to my family's Islamabad house to see Pakeeza and her family crying as they watched nonstop Pakistani cable coverage of the bomb and subsequent blaze. A day later, the cowards at British Airways cancelled their flights to Pakistan.

Remember that I'd had a long history of fleeing Pakistan, going all the way back to when I was four years old and tried to scramble back to the plane that brought us to Karachi. I often feared being "stuck" in my motherland. Now I was stuck. Almost being killed over Chinese food wasn't my worst nightmare; being unable to leave my homeland was. Heaven help me, I still was a very weak man.

Ferhan surprisingly was as panicked as I was, probably because he was scheduled to perform surgeries in Ohio upon his return. He and I called British Airways offices in the U.S. and had to badger them to find some other airline to honor the commitment they'd made to transport us.

On the brighter side, I squeezed a few moments of media whoredom out of the incident. Frank Buckley, a former schoolmate who anchored an L.A. morning news show, wrote me an email to ask if I was okay and if I had been near the attack. I wrote back, "You'll never believe...." And I ended up doing a three-minute phone interview live from Pakistan. I'd happily escape bombings every day to get on TV (so long as I actually escape).

• • • • • • •

Dad died on September 12, 2008. That seemed symbolic to some of us. A man who loved America and who wanted fellow Pakistanis to understand and appreciate America died one day after a dark anniversary of events caused by those who hated America.

Mom saw a different significance. She noted that he died on a Friday, the holiest day of the Muslim week, during the holy month of Ramadan, and she and many others marveled at how God grants only special persons the privilege of passing from this world on such an occasion. Dad wasn't the strictest sort of Muslim, but he was as generous and kind as anyone that his family had known. "That's what counts to God," Mom said.

Given how our world is so shattered by religious divisions, it would be wonderful if that were what counted to the rest of us too.

Acknowledgments

I wish it were easier to express adequately my gratitude to the many people who've encouraged, exhorted, shaped and challenged me, with this book being just one result.

My family members—Mom, Ferhan, Pakeeza, Shabi and Maria—were obviously pivotal in helping me understand and illustrate my journey, and I thank each of them for their grace and patience with me through so many dizzying phases of the moon and of life.

Christian Camozzi coached me for years before serving as my eagle-eyed editor for this project. Thanks, too, to my little brain-trust. Tim Chambers, Dan Cray, Lori Putnam, Pam Nguyen-Hansen and Andrew Whitelock were pivotal advisers in recent years. Tim's and Lori's constructive feedback on early drafts meant a great deal to me. And Liza Molina and Graye Smith served as my brilliant graphic gurus.

At USC, Warren Bennis' mentoring and counsel have been of incalculable value to me in my efforts to "find my voice," personally and professionally. I was privileged to learn at the feet of Steven B. Sample for years. C. L. Max Nikias nurtured my growth and inspired me. Martha Harris gave me invaluable professional opportunities. Debra Ono polished my rough spots and taught me to use my "inside voice." And Varun Soni in USC's Office of Religious Life came along as a godsend, or Vishnu-send, as a friend and collaborator.

Elisa Wiefel Schreiber is the savvy super-strategist who gave me a crucial kick in the right direction. Tim Knight and Joanne and Eric Weidman guided me skillfully in our many discussions. And Jessica Del Mundo, Meilani Lenart and Anne Sage are the "PRos" to whom I'm indebted.

Acknowledgments

It was Karin Levine who first taught me to believe in my writing. And before I'd been published in thirty newspapers around the world, Tanja Lindstrom King, my editor from the days of that wicked Mortar newsletter, helped show how my writing could reach a large audience. Dear friends Ann and Mickey Corcoran heartened me by stashing away early drafts of my writing in hopes that they could someday sell them on eBay, and I can only hope that I and eBay bidders can someday fulfill their peculiar dreams.

Big thanks to Sherine Badawi Walton, Lisa Larsen, Phil Seib and Nick Cull of USC's Center for Public Diplomacy for the chance to work alongside them in their important work. I tip my hat to USC's Alumni Park, for offering a view ideal for inspiring a new day of writing. And I salute the Trojan gang that has been so helpful for so many years—including Ariel Carpenter, Vickie Webb, Bryce Nelson, Joanne Ramirez, Holly Bridges, Scott Mory, Geoff Baum, Geneva Overholser, Geoff Cowan, Richard Dekmejian, Daniel Good, James Vasquez, Eric Mankin, Beth Garrett, Denzil Suite, Courtney Surls, Dennis Cornell, Christine Murakami, Kathleen Bonagofsky, Ben Malcolmson, Lori Meeks, Carl Marziali, Jerome Hughes, Jeremy Schoenberg, Krisztina Holly, Jerrold Green, Ernie Wilson, Tim Burgess, Jennifer Grodsky, Phil Channing, Kevin Starr, and Carola Weil.

From the old Hollywood crowd, I have so many to thank. Matt Mancini, Eleanor Herbst, Andrew and Janna Philpot, Sandra Mader, Carolyn and Mike Malconian, Steve Norris, Lisa and Bill Maier and Laura Robinson have stood close by, and I am grateful for this confirmation that good relationships are stronger than any theology. Among the countless others, I thank Morgan and Veronica Murray, Scott and Lisa Andrews, Shay Case, Steve Tamura, Susan Rigby, Tom Provost and Tod Bolsinger.

I thank Robert Whitcomb of the Providence Journal, Mike Tipping of the Orange County Register and Chris Weinkopf and Mariel Garza of the Daily News of Los Angeles for the opportunities to craft my ideas relating to politics and religion.

Big thanks to the dynamic CAMPUSPEAK team in Aurora, Colorado, led by Amy Butler, Liz Frommelt, TJ Sullivan, Darci Meyer, Felix Sanchez and Tiffanee Hopf.

Acknowledgments

Rachel Dowen's support for this project has been particularly meaningful to me. I also thank a select group of sages, including Jeff Lazenby, Dave Cordero, Yvette Busot, Grant Albrecht, Arielle Fleisher, Ross Andersen, Jonathan Dobrer, Victor Wright, Kitty Felde, Rusty Dornin, Chris Macabuhay, Stacy Whitelock, Frank Buckley, Raph Worrick, Alan Greene, Encarnita Adea, Zeyra Mackey, Nicole Kusano, Alanna Darling, Larry Moretti, Julie Bogart, Rusty Dornin, Mike Chinoy, Shamila Chaudhary, and Mahnaz Fancy. And how could I forget "Dutch," Denton Z. Holland?

I owe a massive debt to Jim MacCuish, who helped me more truly become myself, despite the prevailing sense that the world needed none of that.

Endless and eternal gratitude are owed and freely given to my heroes—Jimmy Page, Robert Plant, John Bonham and John Paul Jones—for providing a soundtrack that made life not just bearable but thrilling during the past three decades of journeying from, oh, Kashmir to Karachi to Camarillo or thereabouts.

Finally, I thank the great Kat Gautreaux and the folks at Wheatmark for their support and wonderful guidance. They have been a pleasure to work with on my first book!

LaVergne, TN USA
25 August 2010
194614LV00003B/148/P